Table of Contents

O9-AHT-553

Unit 2

	Family Times	Phonics	High-Frequency Words	Comprehension	Grammar	Vocabulary	Research and Study Skills	Phonics Review	Spelling	Selection Test	Writing Process
Zoom In!											
The Ugly Duckling / Duck	83-84	85-86	87	88	89, 94	90	91	92, 97	93, 98	95-96	
Eye Spy / Seeing	99-100	101-102	103	104	105, 109	106		107, 113	108, 114	111, 112	
Furry Mouse / Two Mice	115-116	117-118	119	120	121, 125	122		123, 129	124, 130	127-128	
The Old Gollywampus / Snakes	131-132	133-134	135	136	137, 141	138		139, 145	140, 146	143-144	
Spiders Up Close / Anansi and the Talking Melon	147-148	149-150	151	152	153, 158	154		155, 161	156, 162	159-160	157, 163

Unit 3

	Family Times	Phonics	High-Frequency Words	Comprehension	Grammar	Vocabulary	Research and Study Skills	Phonics Review	Spelling	Selection Test	Writing Process
Side By Side											
How I Beat the Giants / Play Ball	165-166	167-168	169	170	171, 175	172		173, 179	174, 180	177-178	
The Storykeeper / People, People, Everywhere!	181-182	183-184	185	186	187, 191	188		189, 195	190, 196	193-194	
New Best Friends / Wanted: Best Friend	197-198	199-200	201	202	203, 207	204		205, 211	206, 212	209-210	
Four Clues for Chee Young Cam / Jansen and the Dinosaur Game	213-214	215-216	217	218	219, 224	220	221	222, 227	223, 228	225-226	
A Good Laugh for Cookie / Moonbear's Pet	229-230	231-232	233	234	235, 240	236		237, 243	238, 244	241-242	239, 245

Family Times

Franny and Ginny   Daddy, Could I Have an Elephant?

What We Like

We like to splash . . . .
And swim all day . . . .
We like to throw . . . .
Our ball and play . . . .

We like to snack . . . .
On three fresh plums
We drink some milk . . . .
Then tap our drums . . . .

We like to clap . . . .
And play guitars . . . .
We like to sleep . . . .
Under the stars . . . .

This rhyme includes words your child is working with in school: words with short *a*, *i*, and *u* vowel sounds (*splash*, *drink*, *drums*) and blends with *l*, *r*, and *s* (*play*, *fresh*, *stars*). Sing "What We Like" with your child, and then make a list of things your family likes to do.

(fold here)

Name: _____

You are your child's first and best teacher!

Here are ways to help your child practice skills while having fun!

Day 1   Look through magazines and newspapers with your child, and cut out simple words that begin with *l*, *r*, and *s* blends. These are words like *block*, *drop*, or *spoon*. Glue the words on separate sheets of paper labeled with the individual blends such as *bl*, *cl*, *fl*, *pl*, *cr*, *dr*, *gr*, *st*, *sm*, *sn*, and so on.

Day 2   Ask your child to write or tell you a story in which he or she is the main character. Have your child include the following words the children are learning to read: *could*, *have*, *need*, *then*, *was*.

Day 3   Before reading a story together, tell your child the name of the story and have him or her look through the illustrations. Ask your child to predict what the story will be about.

Day 4   Ask your child to say or write sentences about himself or herself and draw pictures to match the sentences.

Day 5   Have your child tell you about something that he or she likes to do. Remind your child to use full sentences when speaking.

Read with your child EVERY DAY!

Spin, Read, and Rhyme

Materials paper circle, white paper, pencil, paper clip, 1 button per player

Game Directions

1. Make a simple spinner as shown.

2. Players take turns spinning the spinner and moving their buttons on the gameboard.

3. The player reads the word on the space and says a rhyming word.

4. The first player to reach the end wins!

1	2
3	3
3	1

Start

| tin | bun | rat |
| | | tan |

tub	pit	pal	sun
man			
cub	ram	luck	run
			fin
fish	miss	rib	nap
bit			
kiss	mat	fun	jam
		but	
			End

Say the word for each picture.
Write a, i, or **u** to finish each word.

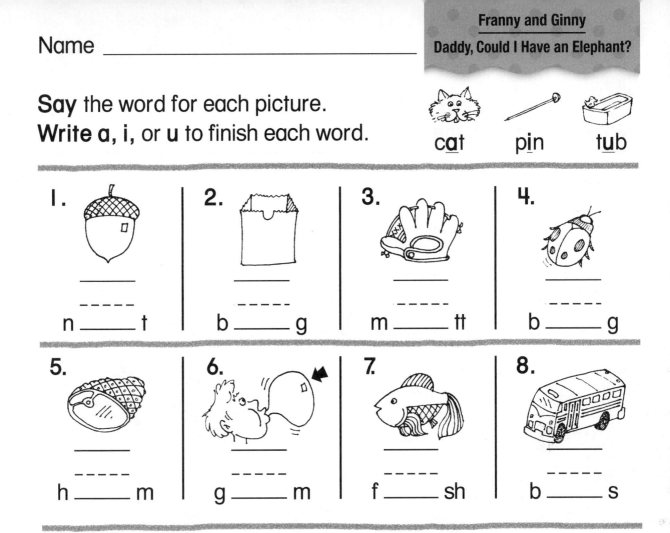

c<u>a</u>t   p<u>i</u>n   t<u>u</u>b

1. n ____ t

2. b ____ g

3. m ____ tt

4. b ____ g

5. h ____ m

6. g ____ m

7. f ____ sh

8. b ____ s

Draw a picture for each word.

9. rug

10. pig

Notes for Home: Your child identified words with the short *a* sound in *mat,* the short *i* sound in *win,* and the short *u* sound in *luck.* **Home Activity:** Work with your child to write a story using the words pictured above.

Circle a word to finish each sentence.
Write the word on the line.

star

1. grabs   grins

   He _____ his things.

2. drives   drips

   Al's dad _____ .

3. spring   splash

   Al makes a big _____ .

4. grin   glad

   Al's _____ is big.

5. swim   smell

   Al likes to _____ .

Notes for Home: Your child wrote words with *l, r,* and *s* blends. **Home Activity:** Look through a children's dictionary with your child to see how many words begin with the following blends: *bl, cl, fl, gl, pl, sl, br, cr, dr, fr, gr, pr, tr, sc, sk, sm, sn, sp, st, sw,* and *str*.

4 **Phonics:** *l, r,* and *s* **Blends**

Level 2.1

© Scott Foresman 2

Pick a word from the box to finish each sentence.
Write the word on the line.

could	have	need	then	was

1. Bess _____ sad.

2. "I _____ a pet," she said.

3. "I _____ get a hippo."

4. "You can _____ a cat," her dad said.

5. _____ Bess was happy.

Notes for Home: This week your child is learning to read the words *could, have, need, then,* and *was*. **Home Activity:** Write these words on slips of paper. Take turns picking a word and using it in a sentence.

Read the sentences and **look** at the pictures.
Follow the directions.

Kelly is a good ball player.
Wade passes Kelly the ball.

1. Circle the sentence that tells what will happen next.

   Kelly will not score.   Kelly will score.

2. Draw a picture to show what you think will happen next.

Chad missed the bus to the game.
Mike's mom stops to give him a ride.

3. Circle the sentence that tells what will happen next.

   Chad will get in the car.   Chad will walk home.

4. Draw a picture to show where Chad will go next.

Notes for Home: Your child made predictions about what will happen next in a story.
Home Activity: Read the beginning of a story with your child. Ask your child to tell you what
he or she thinks will happen next. Then read on to find out if the prediction came true.

A **sentence** is a group of words that tells a complete idea.

This is a sentence: Jon likes to play ball.
This is not a sentence: To play.

Read each group of words.
Write S if the words make a complete sentence.
Write N if the words do **not** make a complete sentence.

S 1. Pam ran to the game.

N 2. Met Flo there.

N 3. Pam and Flo.

S 4. Pam passed the ball to Flo.

Write a complete sentence about Pam and Flo.

5. Pam got the ball before flo got it in the goal.

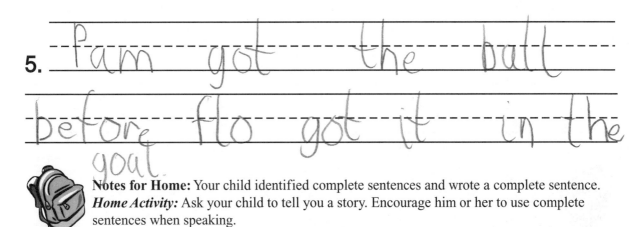

Notes for Home: Your child identified complete sentences and wrote a complete sentence.
Home Activity: Ask your child to tell you a story. Encourage him or her to use complete sentences when speaking.

© Scott Foresman 2

Name _____

Pick a word from the box to match each clue.
Write the word on the line.

apartment	could	elephant	have
need	pianos	quiet	then

1. _____

2. _____

3. hold or own

_____

4. Dogs _____ water.

_____

5. not loud

_____

6. a place to live

_____

7. was able to

_____

8. next

_____

Notes for Home: Your child wrote words that he or she learned to read this week.
Home Activity: Work with your child to write a story using as many of these words as possible.

Name _____

Say the word for each picture.
Write g or **c** to finish each word.

gerbil   **c**ircus

1.

_____ iant

2.

_____ ircle

3.

_____ iraffe

4.

_____ em

5.

_____ ym

6.

_____ ent

7.

_____ ereal

8.

_____ eiling

Find the word that has the same beginning sound as the picture.
Mark the space to show your answer.

9. ⬭ get
   ⬭ germ
   ⬭ give

10. ⬭ center
    ⬭ crib
    ⬭ cat

Notes for Home: Your child reviewed words with initial consonants *g* and *c* with the consonant sounds heard in *gerbil* and *circus*. **Home Activity:** Help your child use each word beginning with *g* or *c* above in a sentence.

| bat | that | fit | this | cub | mug |

Write the word from the box that rhymes with each word below.

1. rug

_____

- - - - - - - - - - - -

_____

2. tub

_____

- - - - - - - - - - - -

_____

3. hit

_____

- - - - - - - - - - - -

_____

4. hiss

_____

- - - - - - - - - - - -

_____

Write two words from the box that rhyme with **cat**.

5.

_____

- - - - - - - - - - - -

_____

6.

_____

- - - - - - - - - - - -

_____

Pick a word from the box to finish each sentence.
Write the word on the line.

| could | have |

_____

- - - - - - - - - - - -

7. I asked my dad if I _____ get a gerbil.

_____

- - - - - - - - - - - -

8. We _____ gerbils in my classroom at school.

Notes for Home: Your child spelled words with the short *a, i,* and *u* sound *(bat, fit,* and *cub)* and two frequently used words: *could, have.* **Home Activity:** Say each spelling word. Have your child use it in a sentence. Say the word again and have your child write it down.

Name _____

Match words from column A with words from column B to make complete sentences.
Write the sentences on the lines.

A
Sid wanted
He went
Sid
It
He named

B
got a fish.
to a pet store.
a new pet.
was a big fish.
it Jaws.

1. _____

2. _____

3. _____

4. _____

5. _____

Notes for Home: Your child combined words to form complete sentences.
Home Activity: Have your child write a story about an animal that would make an interesting pet. Remind your child to use complete sentences.

© Scott Foresman 2

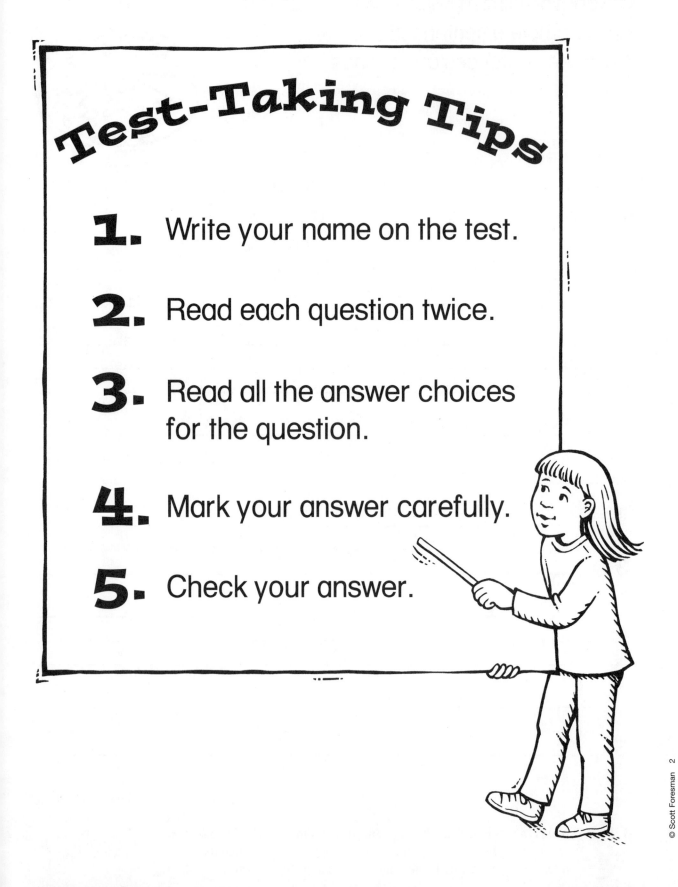

Test-Taking Tips

1. Write your name on the test.

2. Read each question twice.

3. Read all the answer choices for the question.

4. Mark your answer carefully.

5. Check your answer.

Part I: Vocabulary

Find the word that best fits in each sentence.
Mark the space for your answer.

1. Sam saw the _____ at the zoo.
   ⬭ trap   ⬭ must   ⬭ elephant

2. Lin will _____ some pie.
   ⬭ could   ⬭ slip   ⬭ have

3. Will you please be _____ ?
   ⬭ apartment   ⬭ are   ⬭ quiet

4. Dan and Ben are good _____ .
   ⬭ pianos   ⬭ company   ⬭ running

5. Do I _____ a hat?
   ⬭ hear   ⬭ then   ⬭ need

GO ON ➤

Part 2: Comprehension

Read each question.
Mark the space for your answer.

6. What is Daddy doing at first?
   - ⬭ eating
   - ⬭ sleeping
   - ⬭ jumping

7. What kind of pet will Tony get?
   - ⬭ a bird
   - ⬭ a whale
   - ⬭ a dog

8. Tony asks for a —
   - ⬭ sheep.
   - ⬭ piano.
   - ⬭ tub.

9. Why isn't an elephant a good pet for Tony?
   - ⬭ It talks too much.
   - ⬭ It likes to play.
   - ⬭ It is too big.

10. This story is mostly about —
    - ⬭ playing a game.
    - ⬭ getting a pet.
    - ⬭ feeding the elephants.

Name _____

o**ff**   gra**ss**   do**ll**   mi**tt**

Pick a word from the box to match each picture.
Write the word on the line.

| ball | bill | cliff | cuff | dress | glass | kiss | mutt |

1. _____

2. _____

3. _____

4. _____

5. _____

6. _____

7. _____

8. _____

Find the word that has the same ending sound as the picture.
Mark the space to show your answer.

9. ⬭ stiff
   ⬭ miss
   ⬭ cup

10. ⬭ class
    ⬭ grind
    ⬭ tall

 Notes for Home: Your child reviewed words ending with the double consonants *ff, ss, ll,* and *tt.* **Home Activity:** Describe a word on this page and ask your child to guess the word. (For example: *This is something you throw.* Answer: *A ball.*)

| bat | that | fit | this | cub | mug |

Pick a word from the box to finish each sentence.
Write the word on the line.

1. Get the ball and _____ .

2. Does the mitt _____ your hand?

Pick a word from the box to finish each rhyme.
Write the word on the line.

3. Did you see _____?

   It was a black cat.

4. Did you see a _____?

   It was in the tub.

5. What is _____?

   It is just a kiss.

6. Look in the _____ .

   I see a bug.

Write the word from the box that fits in each puzzle.

7.

| could | have |

8.

Notes for Home: Your child spelled words with short vowels *a, i,* and *u* and two frequently
used words: *could, have.* **Home Activity:** Together, make up a story using the spelling words.
Write it but leave blanks for the spelling words. Ask your child to fill in the blanks.

Family Times

Wobbly People/Block House   **Poppleton and the Grapefruit**

Let's Get Along

Let's get along. It's not hard to do,
If you help me, and I help you.
Let's lend a hand. Let's make the bed.
Let's paint the fence and paint the shed.
Let's lend a hand. Let's feed our pet.
Let's wash the pots. Let's not get wet.

Let's lend a hand. Let's dust and mop.
Let's make a list. Let's go and shop.
Let's stop our jobs. It's time to rest.
We get along. We do our best.
We get along. It's not hard to do,
When you help me, and I help you.

This rhyme includes words your child is working with in school: words with the short *e* sound (b*e*d), words with the short *o* sound (m*o*p), and words with final consonant blends (*along, help, hand, paint, list*). Sing "Let's Get Along" with your child. Act out the song as you sing.

(fold here)

Name: _____

You are your child's first and best teacher!

Here are ways to help your child practice skills while having fun!

Day 1   Write a simple short *e* word, such as *red*. Have your child change one letter to make a new word with a short *e* sound, such as *bed*. Take turns changing *bed* to *beg*, and so on. Repeat the activity with a short *o* word, such as *log*.

Day 2   Ask your child to write or say a funny story that uses any of the following words the children are learning to read: *live, made, people, taste, your*.

Day 3   After you read a story to your child, ask who the characters are. Then ask your child to tell you one or two things about each character.

Day 4   Ask your child to say or write sentences about people or objects in your home. Then have him or her identify the subject of each sentence—who or what the sentence is about.

Day 5   Draw pictures of people who are important to your child. Help your child write a complete sentence to go with each picture.

Read with your child EVERY DAY!

Phonics Go Fish

Materials index cards, markers, or crayons

Game Directions

1. Use index cards to make a set of word cards and matching picture cards as shown on page 3.

2. Use 2 players. Mix cards and give each player four cards. Place the remaining cards face down in a pile.

3. Each player takes turns asking another player for a card matching one he or she is holding.

4. If another player does not have a matching card, the player must choose one from the pile.

5. Play until one player has no cards left in his or her hand. The player with the most pairs wins!

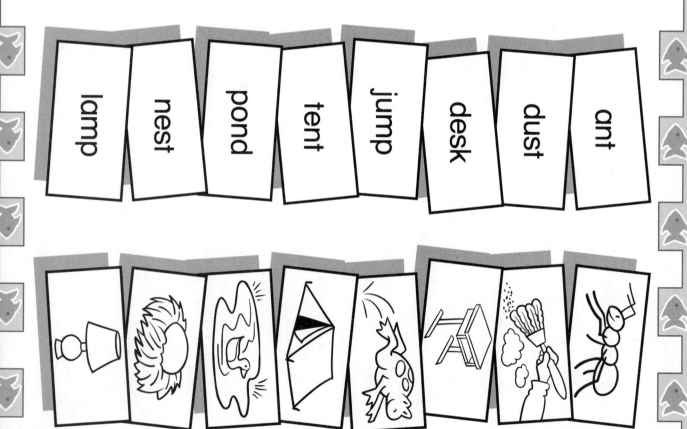

lamp

nest

pond

tent

jump

desk

dust

ant

Name _____

Say the word for each picture.
Write **e** or **o** to finish each word.

b<u>e</u>d   s<u>o</u>ck

1. h __ n

2. n __ t

3. d __ g

4. bl __ ck

5. t __ nt

6. m __ n

7. d __ sk

8. m __ p

9. fr __ g

10. p __ t

Notes for Home: Your child wrote words with the short *e* sound in *bed* and the short *o* sound in *sock*. **Home Activity:** Work with your child to write a story upsing the words pictured above.

© Scott Forseman 2

Name _____

Say the word for each picture.
Write the letters from the box to finish each word.

ant

| ld | nd | sk | st | mp | nt |

1. de _____

2. la _____

3. chi _____

4. te _____

5. co _____

6. ju _____

7. ba _____

8. ne _____

9. sa _____

10. ce _____

Notes for Home: Your child completed words that end with the consonant blends *ld, nd, sk, st, mp,* and *nt.* **Home Activity:** Ask your child to find objects in your home with names that end with these blends. Together, write their names and draw pictures of the objects.

20 **Phonics: Final Consonant Blends**

Level 2.1

© Scott Foresman 2

Pick a word from the box to finish each sentence.
Write the word on the line.

| live | made | people | taste | your |

1. I _____ by a baker.

2. _____ go to his shop.

3. They _____ his rolls.

4. He _____ rolls for us.

5. Here is _____ roll.

Notes for Home: This week your child is learning to read the words *live, made, people, taste,* and *your.* **Home Activity:** Write these words on slips of paper and have your child practice reading them aloud to you.

Name _____

Read the story.
Follow the directions.
Answer the question.

The Park

Bill and Deb like to go to the park.

Bill sits on a bench and reads his book. Then he makes a big castle in the sandbox. Bill likes to sit still.

Deb plays on the swings. She runs and yells. She plays on the slide. Deb does *not* like to sit still.

After they finish playing, Bill and Deb ride their bikes home.

1. Circle the names of the two characters in the story.

2. Put one line under the sentences that tell what Bill does.

3. Put two lines under the sentences that tell what Deb does.

   _____
   _ _ _ _ _ _ _ _ _ _ _ _ _ _

4. Are you more like Bill or Deb? _____

5. Think of other things Bill and Deb might like to do. Draw pictures to show your ideas.

Deb	**Bill**

Notes for Home: Your child identified things that the characters in a story like to do.
Home Activity: Read a story to your child. Ask him or her to identify the characters and to tell one or two things about each one.

22 *Character*

Name _____

The **subject** tells who or what does something.
The subject of this sentence is **man**.

The **man** fixed our door

Underline the subject in each sentence.
Draw a line from each sentence to the picture it matches.

1. The cat ran away.

6.

2. Luke went to look for it.

7.

3. Patty went to help Luke.

8.

4. The cat was stuck in a tree.

9.

5. The children helped the cat.

10.

Notes for Home: Your child identified subjects in sentences and matched each sentence to a
picture. **Home Activity:** With your child, take turns saying simple sentences about something
family members like to do. Then identify the subjects in the sentences.

Pick a word from the box to match each clue.
Write the word on the line.

hundred	knocked	outside
sick	taste	tears

1. eat a little bit

_____

- - - - - - - - - - - -

_____

2. not inside

_____

- - - - - - - - - - - -

_____

3.

_____

- - - - - - - - - - - -

_____

4.

_____

- - - - - - - - - - - -

_____

5. not well

_____

- - - - - - - - - - - -

_____

6. what you get when you cry

_____

- - - - - - - - - - - -

_____

Notes for Home: Your child used clues to write words that he or she learned to read this week. **Home Activity:** Work with your child to write a story using as many of the listed words as possible.

<u>c</u>one   <u>ki</u>te   clo<u>ck</u>

Say the word for each picture.
Write c, k, or **ck** to finish each word.

1. _____ orn

2. _____ itchen

3. _____ id

4. so _____

5. bla _____

6. du _____

7. _____ ab

8. _____ ast

Find the word that has the same beginning sound as the picture.
Mark the space to show your answer.

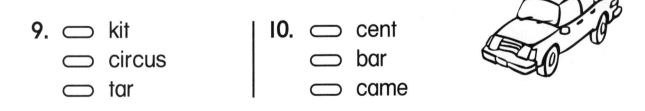

9. ⬭ kit
   ⬭ circus
   ⬭ tar

10. ⬭ cent
    ⬭ bar
    ⬭ came

Notes for Home: Your child reviewed words with the consonants *c, k,* and *ck,* such as *cone,* *kite,* and *clock.* **Home Activity:** Have your child use words with the consonants shown above in a sentence.

| sand | land | send | desk | lost | last |

Write the words from the box that end with each pair of letters.

sk   1. _____

st   2. _____   3. _____

nd   4. _____   5. _____   6. _____

Pick a word from the box to finish each sentence.
Write the word on the line.

7. Did you _____ Ned a letter?

8. I sent it _____ week.

Pick a word from the box to match each picture.
Write the word on the line.

| taste |
| people |

9. _____

10. _____

Notes for Home: Your child spelled words that end with *nd, sk,* and *st* and two frequently used words: *taste, people.* **Home Activity:** Say each spelling word twice. Have your child spell it aloud and use it in a sentence.

Name _____

Part I: Vocabulary

Find the word that best fits in each sentence.
Mark the space for your answer.

1. Who _____ on the wall?
   - ⬭ quiet
   - ⬭ need
   - ⬭ knocked

2. Greg took a _____ of the cake.
   - ⬭ taste
   - ⬭ company
   - ⬭ tears

3. After he ate, he went _____ .
   - ⬭ help
   - ⬭ outside
   - ⬭ apartment

4. He jumped up and down one _____ times.
   - ⬭ could
   - ⬭ quiet
   - ⬭ hundred

5. "Oh, I feel _____ ," said Greg.
   - ⬭ have
   - ⬭ sick
   - ⬭ song

GO ON ➤

Name _____

Part 2: Comprehension

Read each question.

Mark the space for your answer.

6. What does Poppleton do first?
   - ⬭ He goes to the store.
   - ⬭ He eats some grapefruit.
   - ⬭ He watches TV.

7. Why does Poppleton get some grapefruit?
   - ⬭ He wants to live a long time.
   - ⬭ He is sick.
   - ⬭ He wants to make his lips go away.

8. Where does most of this story take place?
   - ⬭ at school
   - ⬭ in Poppleton's house
   - ⬭ outside

9. Who is very old?
   - ⬭ Poppleton
   - ⬭ Uncle Bill
   - ⬭ Hudson

10. What can you tell about Poppleton from this story?
    - ⬭ He does not like grapefruit.
    - ⬭ He eats too much.
    - ⬭ He has no friends.

Pick a blend from the box to finish each word.
Write the blend on the line.

bl   cr   dr   fr   gr   sp   st   thr

<u>gr</u>ape<u>fr</u>uit

1. _____ apes

2. _____ one

3. _____ ess

4. _____ og

5. _____ ab

6. _____ ock

7. _____ ider

8. _____ ee

Find the word that has the same beginning blend as the picture.
Mark the space to show your answer.

9. ⭕ trunk
　　 ⭕ three
　　 ⭕ bee

10. ⭕ press
　　 ⭕ flop
　　 ⭕ spill

Notes for Home: Your child reviewed blends using *l, r,* and *s* as in <u>block</u>, <u>crab</u>, and *spoon*.
Home Activity: Work with your child to write words with *l, r,* and *s* blends on separate index
cards. Illustrate these words on other cards. Have your child match words and pictures.

© Scott Foresman 2

Name _____

sand	land	send	desk	lost	last

Write the word from the box that means the opposite of each word below.

1. first

   _____

   - - - - - - - - -

   _____

2. found

   _____

   - - - - - - - - -

   _____

3. get

   _____

   - - - - - - - - -

   _____

Write two words from the box that rhyme with **hand**.

4. _____

   - - - - - - - - -

   _____

5. _____

   - - - - - - - - -

   _____

Write a word from the box to match the picture.

6. _____

   - - - - - - - -

   _____

Pick a word from the box to finish each sentence.
Write the word on the line.

taste

people

7. I like the _____ of grapefruit.

   _____

   - - - - - - - - - -

8. Some _____ eat it every day.

   _____

   - - - - - - - - - -

Notes for Home: Your child spelled words that end with *nd, sk,* and *st* and two frequently used words: *taste, people.* **Home Activity:** Work with your child to write a short story that uses the spelling words. Encourage your child to use as many pf the words as possible.

© Scott Foresman 2

Family Times

Tools

The Workers

What Will They Make?

Pete will use his tools to make
One delicious chocolate cake.
Pete will make it taste so nice.
There are cherries in each slice.

Pete will place it on a plate.
Then he'll share it. Don't be late!
Rose will use her tools to make
One white shed down by the lake.

Rose will make it in the shade.
She will work until it's made.
Rose will place her bike inside.
When it's time, she'll take a ride.

This rhyme includes words your child is working with in school: words with long vowels with final *e (make, nice)*, and words that begin with *ch, th, sh,* and *wh.* Sing "What Will They Make?" along with your child. As you sing the rhyme, clap your hands for each word with a long vowel sound.

(fold here)

Name: _____

You are your child's first and best teacher!

Here are ways to help your child practice skills while having fun!

Day 1 Write *ch, th, sh,* and *wh* on separate sheets of paper. Work with your child to list words that begin with each pair of letters, such as *cherry, things, share,* and *whale.*

Day 2 Ask your child to write or say sentences that use any of the following words that the children are learning to read: *clean, many, use, work, world.*

Day 3 Before reading a book together, ask your child to look through the illustrations. Then ask your child to make predictions about the mood of the story. (Ask: *Is it happy or sad?*)

Day 4 Ask your child to draw a picture. Then have him or her write one or two sentences to describe what is happening in the picture.

Day 5 Ask your child to tell you about something he or she did in school this week. Encourage your child to use complete sentences when speaking.

Read with your child EVERY DAY!

Cover Up

Materials 1 game card per player,
16 buttons or other game markers per player

Game Directions

1. Use the words below to make game cards for
each player like the one shown. Words should be
in a different order for each card.

2. Write the 16 words below on slips of paper.
Players take turns picking a word and reading
it aloud.

3. Players use buttons to cover the words called.

4. The first player to cover a row of words
across, down, or diagonally wins!

Game Card Words

use, rule, flute, tune, rake, make, plate, shade, bone,
phone, rope, pole, slice, rice, bike, ride

use	rule	flute	tune
rake	make	plate	shade
bone	phone	rope	pole
slice	rice	bike	ride

Name _____

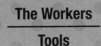 g<u>a</u>te

Say the word for each picture.
Circle the words that have the same long vowel sound.

1.
cube

| mule | prune | mud |
| tube | use | bone |

2.
cake

| plane | brave | cane |
| sale | that | snake |

3.
rope

| rose | hose | stone |
| stop | phone | slope |

4.
kite

| pile | dime | slide |
| shine | kit | drip |

5.
nose

| hose | bone | flop |
| not | froze | poke |

 Notes for Home: Your child identified words with long vowel sounds that follow the pattern consonant-vowel-consonant-*e (cube, cake, robe, kite, nose)*. **Home Activity:** Work with your child to write sentences using the long-vowel words listed above.

Name _____

Say the word for each picture.
Write the letters from the box to finish each word.

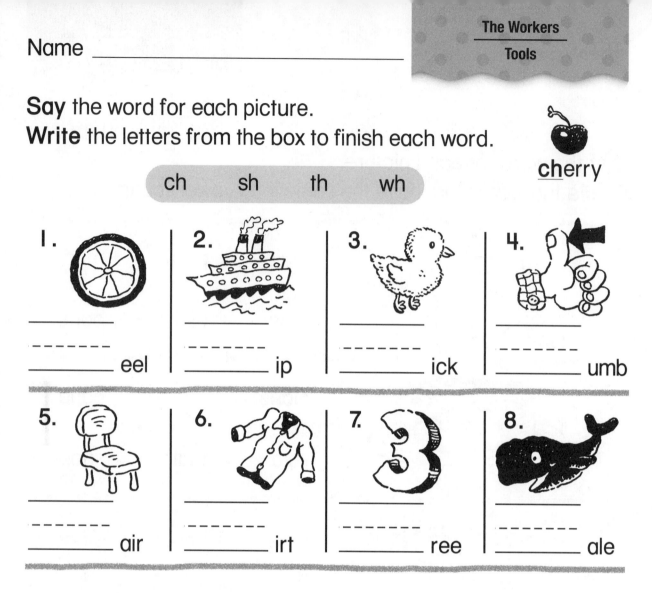

<u>ch</u>erry

ch   sh   th   wh

1. _____ eel

2. _____ ip

3. _____ ick

4. _____ umb

5. _____ air

6. _____ irt

7. _____ ree

8. _____ ale

Draw a picture for each word.

9. child

10. shark

Notes for Home: Your child completed words that begin with the consonants *ch, th, wh,* and *sh.* **Home Activity:** Point to the words your child completed. Have your child read each word aloud.

36 **Phonics: Initial Consonant Digraphs**

Level 2.1

Name _____

Pick a word from the box to finish each sentence.
Write the word on the line. Use each word only once.

| clean | many | use | work | world |

1. There are _____ kinds of tools.

2. Mops and brooms _____ floors.

3. Farmers _____ with tractors.

4. Chefs _____ tools to cook.

5. People around the _____ use tools.

Notes for Home: This week your child is learning to read the words *clean, many, use, work,* and *world.* ***Home Activity:*** Write and show your child these words. Have your child use each word in a sentence and draw a picture to go with it.

Name _____

Read the text below.
Follow the directions.

How to Make a Tree House
by Ted Stone

You can make a tree house.
You need wood, a hammer, a saw,
and nails.
First you build the floor.
Next you build the walls.
Then you put on the roof.
You can paint the tree house if you like.
Then invite your friends to come play!

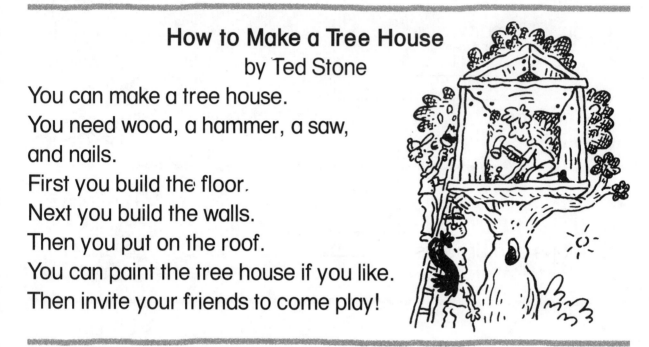

1. Circle the name of the author.

2. Circle the word that tells what the text is all about.

   tree houses   paint   walls

3. Underline the things you need to make a tree house.

4. Circle the part of the tree house that you build first.

5. Tell why you think the author wrote this text.

_____

- -

_____

- -

_____

Notes for Home: Your child wrote about a nonfiction text and told why an author wrote it.
Home Activity: Read a nonfiction article or story to your child. Ask him or her to identify
who wrote the material and tell why the writer may have written it.

Name _____

The **predicate** tells what the subject does.
Opens the can is the predicate.

The man **opens** the **can**.

Look at each picture.
Circle a predicate to finish each sentence.

---

1. The doctor _____ .

   looks in Tim's ear

   checks Tim's nose

---

2. Stan _____ .

   cleans the stove

   washes the car

---

3. Patty _____ .

   rides her bike

   fixes the wheel

---

4. Hal _____ .

   uses a brush

   looks at his paper

---

5. Bob's mom _____ .

   drinks milk

   cuts lemons

Notes for Home: Your child chose a predicate, the part of a sentence that tells what the subject does, to complete each sentence. ***Home Activity:*** Take turns with your child saying simple sentences and identifying the predicate for each sentence.

Name _____

Pick a word from the box to match each clue.
Write the word on the line.

clean   easier   farm   fix   tools   use   world   write

1.

_____

- - - - - - - - - - - - - -

_____

2.

_____

- - - - - - - - - - - - - -

_____

3. what you do to
   something broken

_____

- - - - - - - - - - - - - -

_____

4. what you do to
   something dirty

_____

- - - - - - - - - - - - - -

_____

5. what you do with a tractor

_____

- - - - - - - - - - - - - -

_____

6. what you do with
   a paper and pen

_____

- - - - - - - - - - - - - -

_____

7. not harder

_____

- - - - - - - - - - - - - -

_____

8. We _____ a saw to cut.

_____

- - - - - - - - - - - - - -

_____

Notes for Home: Your child used clues to write vocabulary words that he or she learned to read this week. *Home Activity:* Work with your child to write a story using as many of these words as possible.

Name _____

Read the map.
Follow the directions below.

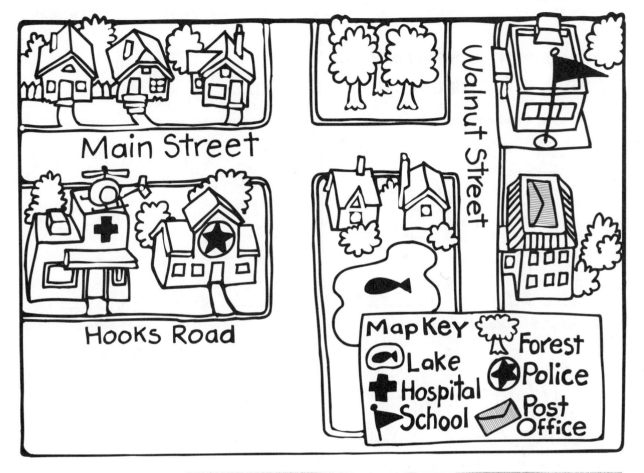

1. Color the lake blue.

2. Color the school red.

3. Circle the name of the street where the hospital is.

4. Draw a path to show how to get from the school to the hospital.

5. Put a box around the name of the street where the post office is.

Notes for Home: Your child practiced reading a simple map. *Home Activity:* Draw a simple map of your neighborhood. Take your child on a walk. Have him or her identify places on the map. Encourage your child to add to the map.

Name _____

b_a_t　　　be_e_d　　　di_i_sh　　　m_o_p　　　bu_u_s

Say the word for each picture.
Write a, e, i, o, or **u** to finish each word.

1. fl ____ g

2. p ____ t

3. f ____ sh

4. pl ____ m

5. t ____ n

6. d ____ ck

7. b ____ lt

8. b ____ b

Find the word that has the same middle sound as the picture.
Mark the space to show your answer.

9. ⬭ drag
　 ⬭ dig
　 ⬭ dog

10. ⬭ boss
　　 ⬭ bank
　　 ⬭ bug

Notes for Home: Your child reviewed words with short vowel sounds as heard in *bat, bed, pig, mop,* and *bus.* **Home Activity:** Say a word with a short vowel sound. Have your child name as many rhyming words as he or she can. Try it with another vowel sound.

Part I: Vocabulary

Find the word that best fits in each sentence.
Mark the space for your answer.

1. They will _____ the boat with water.
   ⬭ write   ⬭ clean   ⬭ fix

2. My job is _____ than yours.
   ⬭ good   ⬭ again   ⬭ easier

3. They _____ on flat land.
   ⬭ farm   ⬭ tools   ⬭ need

4. May I _____ your bike?
   ⬭ read   ⬭ use   ⬭ call

5. We live in a big _____ .
   ⬭ world   ⬭ boy   ⬭ school

GO ON ➡

Part 2: Comprehension

Read each question.
Mark the space for your answer.

6. Which people use tools to dig?
   - ⬭ teachers
   - ⬭ cooks
   - ⬭ farmers

7. From this story, you can tell that —
   - ⬭ only grown-ups use tools.
   - ⬭ tools cost a lot money.
   - ⬭ tools have many uses.

8. The author wrote this story to —
   - ⬭ make fun of people.
   - ⬭ tell about tools.
   - ⬭ teach you to work faster.

9. Which sentence tells what the story is mostly about?
   - ⬭ "Tools help us in many ways."
   - ⬭ "We can even eat with tools!"
   - ⬭ "People use tools to make things."

10. People can use tools when they —
    - ⬭ read books.
    - ⬭ walk.
    - ⬭ fix cars.

Name _____

wi**nd**   wor**ld**   he**lp**   te**nt**

Circle the word for each picture.

1. child   chair

2. bend   bed

3. call   cold

4. gulp   gum

5. play   plant

6. bad   band

7. ant   at

8. cell   cent

Find the word that has the same ending sound as the picture.
Mark the space to show your answer.

9. ⬭ ham
   ⬭ hint
   ⬭ blind

10. ⬭ tall
    ⬭ flap
    ⬭ fold

Notes for Home: Your child reviewed words that end with *ld, lp, nd,* and *nt.* **Home Activity:** Write a word that ends with each of the blends. Have your child build new words by changing the beginning letters, *cold* becomes *mold,* for example.

child   chin   chip   shape   ship   shut

Pick a word from the box to match each picture.
Write the word on the line.

1. _____

2. _____

3. _____

Write three words from the box that have the same beginning
sound as   .

_____   _____   _____

4. _____   5. _____   6. _____

Pick a word from the box to match each clue.
Write the word on the line.

use   world

7. You could see this from a spaceship. _____

8. You _____ tools to fix things. _____

Notes for Home: Your child spelled words that begin with *ch* and *sh* and two frequently used
words: *use, world*. **Home Activity:** Mix up the letters of each spelling word, for example: *ichdl*
for *child*. Have your child unscramble the letters and write the word.

Family Times

The Safety Song

We're the team you need to meet.
We're the team that can't be beat!

Sneakers will protect your feet.
Check your wheels. Check your seat.

Check each tire for a leak.
Practice safety every week.

On a steep hill, watch your speed.
There are signs you need to read.

Bring a drink and lunch along.
Teach each friend this safety song!

This rhyme includes words your child is working with in school: words with the long *e* sound spelled *ee* and *ea* (*meet*, *beat*) and words ending in *ch*, *ng*, *tch*. Read "The Safety Song" aloud together. Find all the long *e* words and sort them by their *ea* or *ee* spellings.

(fold here)

Name: _____

You are your child's first and best teacher!

Here are ways to help your child practice skills while having fun!

Day 1 Write a list of long *e* words spelled *ea* and *ee*, such as *bean, flea, seat, tree, green, three*. Help your child draw pictures for these words and write a sentence for each picture.

Day 2 Ask your child to write or say sentences that use any of the following words that your child is learning to read: *should, their; through, very, would.*

Day 3 After reading a story, ask your child to tell you about the story's setting. Ask questions such as: *Where does the story take place? Does it take place today or a long time ago?*

Day 4 Choose a subject that is particularly interesting to your child, such as a favorite hobby. Take turns asking and answering questions about the subject.

Day 5 Read a nonfiction story to your child, and then discuss it. Encourage him or her to ask thoughtful questions about the subject.

Read with your child EVERY DAY!

Mix and Match

Materials   index cards, markers or crayons

Game Directions

1. Use index cards to make a set of word cards and matching picture cards as shown.

2. Mix the cards and place each card face down. Players take turns choosing two cards to try to find a match.

3. Players keep any matching pairs. If players do not pick a match, they return the cards face down to their original positions.

4. Play until all matches have been made. The player with the most pairs at the end wins!

branch	bench	lunch	fish
dish	wash	moth	teeth
crutch	watch	string	king

Name _____

These bees only fly past words with the **long e** sound.
Draw a line to show the path from the bees to the tree.

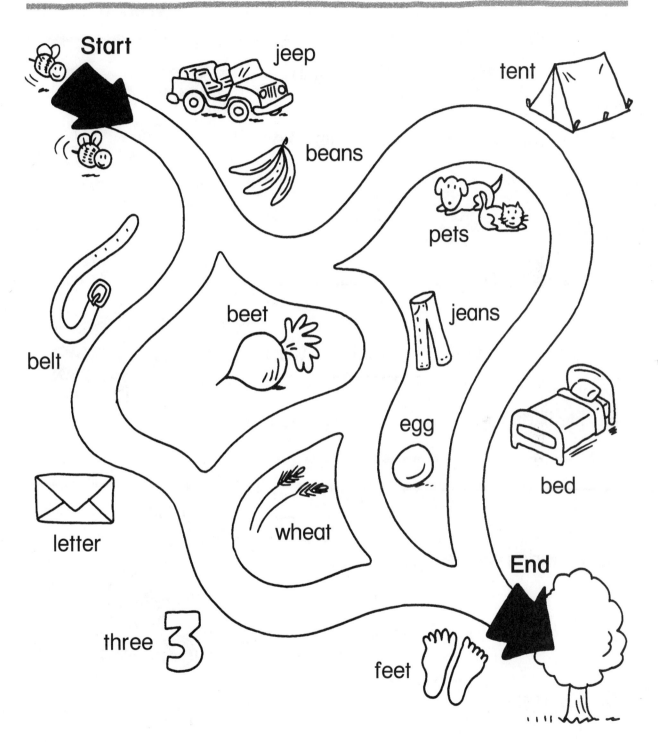

Start

jeep

tent

beans

pets

beet

jeans

belt

egg

bed

letter

wheat

End

three 3

feet

Notes for Home: Your child identified words with long *e* sounds spelled *ea* and *ee* as in *leaf* and *tree*. **Home Activity:** Work with your child to make picture cards of the long *e* words above. Draw a picture on the front of a card and write the word for it on the back.

Circle a word to finish each sentence.
Write the word on the line.

wren**ch**

wash   watch   wish

_____

- - - - - - - - - - - - -

1. Jon will _____ his bike.

lunch   bunch   bench

_____

- - - - - - - - - - - - -

2. He sits on a _____ to eat.

what   watch   wash

_____

- - - - - - - - - - - - -

3. He likes to _____ the birds.

pad   path   pat

_____

- - - - - - - - - - - - -

4. He rides on the _____ .

long   song   son

_____

- - - - - - - - - - - - -

5. He sings a _____ .

Notes for Home: Your child completed sentences by choosing words that end with *th, ch, ng, sh,* or *tch.* **Home Activity:** Read a simple story with your child. As you find words with these endings, ask your child to read the words aloud.

Name _____

Pick a word from the box to finish each sentence.
Write the word on the line.

should	their	through	very	would

_____
1. Jill and Bill ride _____ bikes.

_____
2. They ride _____ the park.

_____
3. They know they _____ always wear helmets.

_____
4. They are _____ safe riders.

_____
5. They _____ like to ride every day.

Notes for Home: This week your child is learning to read the words *should, their, through, very,* and *would.* ***Home Activity:*** Help your child write a story using as many of the words as possible. Draw pictures to illustrate the story.

Name _____

Read each story.
Underline the sentence that tells where the story takes place.
Draw a picture that shows where the story takes place.

1. Last week Anne rode her bike to the animal park. She saw seals and birds. Then she ate a snack.

2.

3. Cal and Ben slept in their backyard. They had a tent. Their mom made them some popcorn and gave them flashlights.

4.

Write the name of a story you have read.
Draw a picture that shows where the story takes place. It can be a real place or make-believe. It can take place now or long ago.

5. _____

Notes for Home: Your child identified the setting of a story. *Home Activity:* Read a story to your child. Ask questions such as: *Is this a real or make-believe place? Is it long ago or now?* Have your child tell you where and when the story takes place.

Name _____

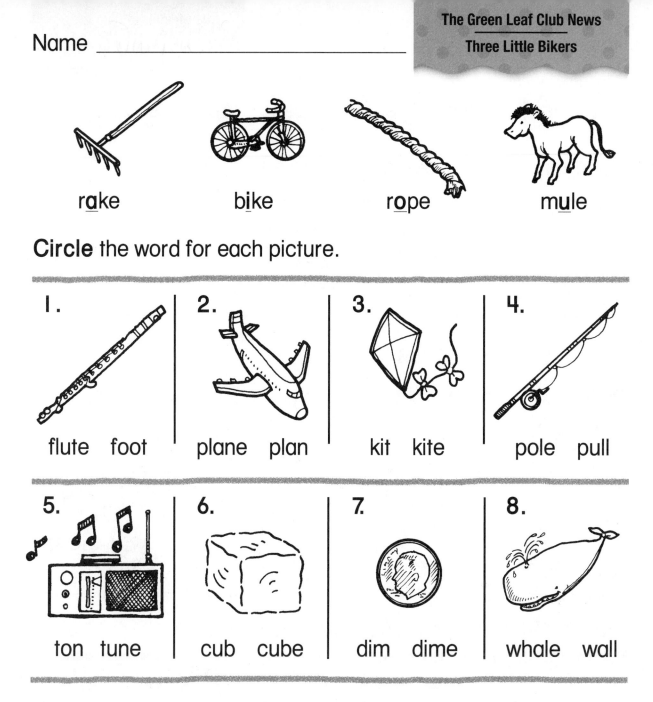

rake   bike   rope   mule

Circle the word for each picture.

1.	2.	3.	4.
flute foot	plane plan	kit kite	pole pull

5.	6.	7.	8.
ton tune	cub cube	dim dime	whale wall

Find the word that has the same vowel sound as the picture.
Mark the space to show your answer.

9. ⬭ nose
   ⬭ not
   ⬭ now

10. ⬭ fill
    ⬭ fit
    ⬭ five

Notes for Home: Your child identified words with long vowels that follow the pattern:
consonant-vowel-consonant-*e*. **Home Activity:** Write *rake, bike, rope,* and *mule.* Challenge
your child to make new long vowel words by changing one or two letters lof each word.

leaf	meal	team	deep	free	seen

Write three words from the box with **ee**.

1. _____   2. _____   3. _____

Write three words from the box with **ea**.

4. _____   5. _____   6. _____

Pick a word from the box to match each clue.
Write the word on the line.

7. _____

8. _____

Pick a word from the box to finish each sentence.
Write the word on the line.

should	their

9. Bikers _____ always wear helmets.

10. Pam and Jake want _____ team to win.

Notes for Home: Your child spelled words with the long *e* vowel sound spelled *ea* and *ee* as in *leaf* and *deep* and two frequently used words: *should, their.* **Home Activity:** Say each spelling word twice. Have your child spell the word aloud.

Part 1: Vocabulary

Find the word that best fits in each sentence.
Mark the space for your answer.

1. I can _____ to the top.
   ⬭ fix   ⬭ climb   ⬭ clean

2. Jim got wet from the _____ of water.
   ⬭ spray   ⬭ world   ⬭ spider

3. Ali _____ at the funny story.
   ⬭ drew   ⬭ took   ⬭ giggled

4. You _____ eat your lunch.
   ⬭ about   ⬭ should   ⬭ long

5. We rode _____ the grass.
   ⬭ through   ⬭ everywhere ⬭ after

GO ON

Part 2: Comprehension

Read each question.
Mark the space for your answer.

6. You can tell at the beginning of the story that —
   - ⬭ it was a nice day.
   - ⬭ a storm was coming.
   - ⬭ it was almost night.

7. What made the bikers' shirts puff out like sails?
   - ⬭ the flags
   - ⬭ the wind
   - ⬭ their packs

8. The tracks in the grass were made by —
   - ⬭ the bikes' tires.
   - ⬭ three little snakes.
   - ⬭ the bikers' feet.

9. Where did the bikers spend most of their time?
   - ⬭ in a puddle
   - ⬭ on the hill
   - ⬭ in a gully

10. What helps the bikers when they ride at night?
    - ⬭ having a flag that flaps
    - ⬭ bringing a lunch
    - ⬭ turning on their headlights

white   **sh**irt   **th**orn   **ch**est

Say the word for each picture.
Write wh, sh, th, or **ch** to finish each word.

1. _____ eep

2. _____ orts

3. _____ eel

4. _____ erry

5. _____ umb

6. _____ imp

7. _____ ovel

8. _____ ale

Find the word that has the same beginning sound as the picture.
Mark the space to show your answer.

9. ○ cheek
   ○ shine
   ○ flip

10. ○ chain
    ○ plane
    ○ green

Notes for Home: Your child reviewed words that begin with *wh, sh, th,* and *ch* as in *whale, shirt, thorn,* and *chest.* **Home Activity:** Ask your child to read aloud the words above that begin with these letter pairs. Together, write a story using some of these words.

| leaf | meal | team | deep | free | seen |

Pick a word from the box to match each picture.
Write the word on the line.

1. _____
   - - - - - - - - - -
   _____

2. _____
   - - - - - - - - - -
   _____

3. _____
   - - - - - - - - - -
   _____

Pick a word from the box to finish each rhyme.
Write the word on the line.

_____
- - - - - - - - - -

4. Please _____ my kite from the tree.

_____
- - - - - - - - - -

5. Have you ever _____ a frog that's not green?

_____
- - - - - - - - - -

6. You don't hear a peep from the fish in the _____ .

Write the word from the box that fits in each puzzle.

| should | their |

7. ☐☐☐☐☐

8. ☐☐☐☐☐☐

Notes for Home: Your child spelled words with long *e* spelled *ee* and *ea* and two frequently used words: *should, their*. **Home Activity:** Read the spelling words to your child. Have him or her write each word down and then use it in a sentence about himself or herself.

Family Times

House Repair

The Surprise

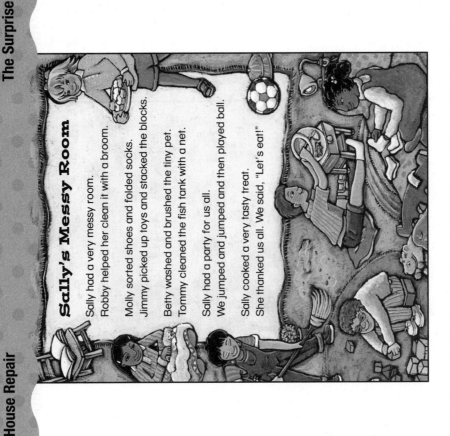

Sally's Messy Room

Sally had a very messy room.
Robby helped her clean it with a broom.

Molly sorted shoes and folded socks.
Jimmy picked up toys and stacked the blocks.

Betty washed and brushed the tiny pet.
Tommy cleaned the fish tank with a net.

Sally had a party for us all.
We jumped and jumped and then played ball.

Sally cooked a very tasty treat.
She thanked us all. We said, "Let's eat!"

This rhyme includes words your child is working with in school: words with the long *e* sound spelled *e* and *y* (*we, party*) and words ending with *-ed* (*jumped*). Sing "Sally's Messy Room" with your child. Act out the song as you sing the words.

(fold here)

Name: _____

You are your child's first and best teacher!

Here are ways to help your child practice skills while having fun!

Day 1 Write a list of long *e* words spelled *e* and *y* such as *we, be, she, happy, very, penny*. Have your child use these words to make up sentences about helping others.

Day 2 Work with your child to write short rhyming sentences that include any of these words: *house, never, off, these, took.*

Day 3 When reading together, encourage your child to use the illustrations to draw conclusions about the characters' feelings and actions. Ask questions such as: *Why is the boy smiling in this picture?*

Day 4 Ask your child to say or write several sentences that tell something interesting about himself or herself.

Day 5 Have your child tell you a simple story. Encourage your child to make up a story with a beginning, middle, and end.

Read with your child EVERY DAY!

Race to the Top

Materials paper circle, pencil, paper clip, 1 button

Game Directions

1. Make a spinner as shown.

2. Each player takes turns spinning the spinner and moving his or her button up a ladder.

3. Player reads the word landed on and uses it in a sentence.

4. The first player who reaches the top of his or her ladder wins!

me
party
penny
she
very
maybe
messy
sandy
windy
dirty

looked
jumped
licked
cooked
stayed
filled
helped
rolled
banged
talked

Underline the word in each sentence that has the **long e** sound.
Write the word on the line.

me   penny

1. Di has a messy room.

2. She wants it to look nice.

3. Bill is happy to help her.

4. He likes to put toys away.

5. Di is lucky to have a pal like Bill.

Notes for Home: Your child identified words with the long *e* sound spelled *e* and *y (me, penny)*. **Home Activity:** Write five simple long *e* words spelled *e* or *y*. Ask your child to read the words to you.

Name _____

Add -ed to the word in ( ).
Write the new word on the line to finish each sentence.

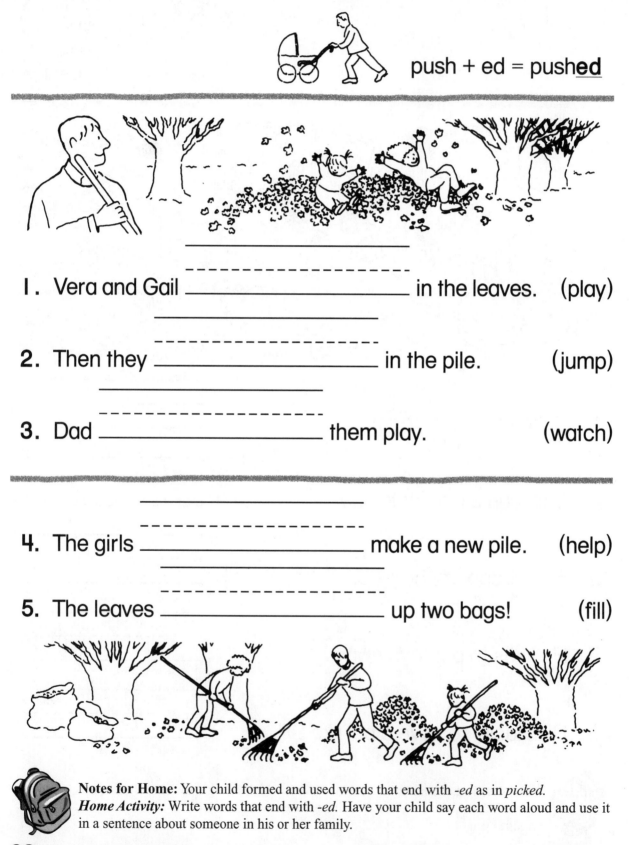

push + ed = push**ed**

1. Vera and Gail _____ in the leaves.   (play)

2. Then they _____ in the pile.   (jump)

3. Dad _____ them play.   (watch)

4. The girls _____ make a new pile.   (help)

5. The leaves _____ up two bags!   (fill)

Notes for Home: Your child formed and used words that end with *-ed* as in *picked.*
Home Activity: Write words that end with *-ed.* Have your child say each word aloud and use it in a sentence about someone in his or her family.

Pick a word from the box to finish each sentence.
Write the word on the line.

house   never   off   these   took

1. _____ leaves are a mess!

2. Greg _____ wants to rake.

3. Becky _____ the rake.

4. Greg gets a bag from the _____ .

5. Now all the leaves are _____ the ground!

Notes for Home: This week your child is learning to read the words *house, never, off, these,*
and *took.* **Home Activity:** Have your child use these words to write or say a story about helping
someone.

© Scott Foresman 2

Look at the picture.
Circle the word that best finishes each sentence.
Write the word on the line.

sad   happy
- - - - - - - - - - - - -
1. The girl is _____ .

book   mom
- - - - - - - - - - - - -
2. She wants her _____ .

sad   happy
- - - - - - - - - - - - -
3. The boy wants to make her _____ .

pencil   toy
- - - - - - - - - - - - -
4. He gives her a _____ .

Write a sentence about how you think the girl feels now.

5. _____

_____

Notes for Home: Your child used text and illustrations to draw conclusions about a story.
Home Activity: As you read a story to your child, stop often to ask your child to think about
what is happening or why a character is doing something.

wished   crossed   jumped   picked   pulled   pushed

Add -ed to each base word below to make a word from the box.
Write the word on the line.

1. push _____

2. pull _____

3. cross _____

4. jump _____

5. wish _____

6. pick _____

Pick a word from the box to finish each sentence.
Write the word on the line.

7. He _____ a flower.

8. She _____ rope.

Pick a word from the box to match each clue.   house never
Write the word on the line.

9. People can live in one of these. _____

10. It means "not ever." _____

Notes for Home: Your child spelled words that end with *-ed* and two frequently used words: *house, never.* **Home Activity:** Say each base word. Have your child add *-ed.*

Circle the word for each picture.   l**ea**f   t**ee**th

1.

beach   bench

2.

bead   bed

3.

suds   seeds

4.

sell   seal

5.

sheep   ship

6.

buns   beans

7.

tree   trip

8.

best   bees

Find the word that has the same middle sound as the picture.
Mark the space to show your answer.

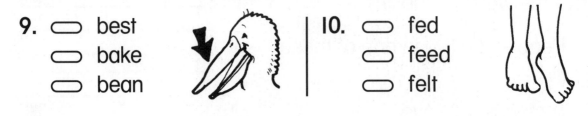

9. ⬭ best
   ⬭ bake
   ⬭ bean

10. ⬭ fed
    ⬭ feed
    ⬭ felt

Notes for Home: Your child reviewed words with long *e* spelled *ea* and *ee* as in *leaf* and *teeth*. **Home Activity:** Write *leaf* and *teeth*. Have your child build new long *e* words by changing some of the consonants, for example, *leaf* becomes *lean* or *leap*.

Part I: Vocabulary

Find the word that best fits in each sentence.
Mark the space for your answer.

1. Jim lives in a big red _____ .
   ⬭ tool   ⬭ never   ⬭ house

2. Did you _____ the right answer?
   ⬭ clean   ⬭ climb   ⬭ guess

3. We will go to the zoo _____ .
   ⬭ tomorrow   ⬭ everywhere   ⬭ perfect

4. Sal put all her toys in a _____ .
   ⬭ pile   ⬭ pleased   ⬭ world

5. Leo was _____ to see a cow in school.
   ⬭ pretty   ⬭ surprised   ⬭ done

GO ON

Part 2: Comprehension

Read each question.

Mark the space for your answer.

6. Frog wanted to surprise Toad because —
   - ⬭ Frog and Toad were friends.
   - ⬭ Frog was mean.
   - ⬭ Frog did not like Toad.

7. Why did Frog run through the woods?
   - ⬭ He wanted to find a new friend.
   - ⬭ He did not want Toad to see him.
   - ⬭ He wanted to see the leaves on the trees.

8. As Frog ran through the woods, Toad was —
   - ⬭ sleeping.
   - ⬭ raking his own yard.
   - ⬭ running to Frog's house.

9. You can tell that both Frog and Toad like to —
   - ⬭ play in piles of leaves.
   - ⬭ help each other.
   - ⬭ sleep late in the morning.

10. Do you think Frog was surprised when he got home?
    - ⬭ Yes, because his front yard was clean.
    - ⬭ No, because he knew Toad had raked his yard.
    - ⬭ No, because the yard looked the same as before.

Name _____

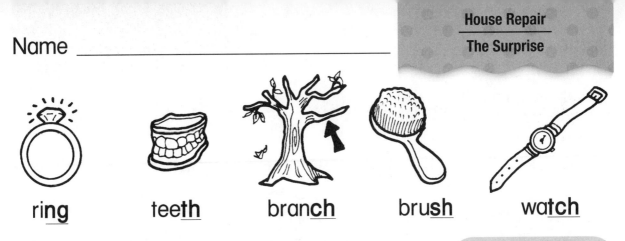

ri**ng**   tee**th**   bran**ch**   bru**sh**   wa**tch**

Pick letters from the box to finish each word.
Write the letters on the line.

ng   th   ch
sh   tch

1.

ba _____

2.

scra _____

3.

in _____

4.

bu _____

5.

di _____

6.

wi _____

7.

ba _____

8.

pi _____

Find the word that has the same ending sound as the picture.
Mark the space to show your answer.

9. ⬭ lash
   ⬭ catch
   ⬭ sing

10. ⬭ fish
    ⬭ reach
    ⬭ path

 Notes for Home: Your child reviewed words that end with *ng, th, ch, sh,* and *tch.* **Home Activity:** Write words that end with these letter combinations on index cards. Hide the cards in your home. When your child finds a card, have him or her read the word aloud.

Name _____

| wished | crossed | jumped | picked | pulled | pushed |

Write a word from the box to match each picture.

1.

2.

3.

_____

- - - - - - - - - - - - - - -

_____

Pick a word from the box to match each clue.
Write the word on the line.

_____

- - - - - - - - - - - - - - -

4. Jo did this when she saw a star.   _____

_____

- - - - - - - - - - - - - - -

5. You did this to get across the street.   _____

_____

- - - - - - - - - - - - - - -

6. Bob's dad did this to Bob's swing.   _____

_____

Pick a word from the box to finish each sentence.
Write the word on the line.

house

never

_____

- - - - - - - - - - - - - - -

7. Vera and her dad live in a big _____ .

_____

- - - - - - - - - - - - - - -

8. She _____ stays home alone.

Notes for Home: Your child spelled words that end with *-ed* and two frequently used words: *house, never.* **Home Activity:** Play charades with your child. One person acts out a spelling word while the other tries to guess and spell it.

© Scott Foresman 2

Correct each sentence.
Write it on the line.
Hint: Each sentence should end with a . , a ? , or an ! .

1. Look at the big dog

_____

- -

_____

2. Is the dog nice

_____

- -

_____

3. The dog barked

_____

- -

_____

4. Go away, cats

_____

- -

_____

5. We must run fast

_____

- -

_____

Notes for Home: Your child corrected sentences by adding end marks. *Home Activity:* Write sentences without end marks on slips of paper. Have your child pick a slip of paper and then rewrite the sentence, adding a question mark, a period, or an exclamation mark.

Words I Can Now Read and Write

_____   _____
-----------------------   -----------------------
_____   _____

_____   _____
-----------------------   -----------------------
_____   _____

_____   _____
-----------------------   -----------------------
_____   _____

_____   _____
-----------------------   -----------------------
_____   _____

                           _____

                           _____

                           _____

                           _____

                           _____

Family Times

The Ugly Duckling

Duck

Changes

There are changes every day.
Night is turning into day.
When the blue sky turns to gray,
Clouds will hide the sun away.
Rain will make the daisies grow.
Rainbows may appear, you know!

There are changes every day.
April's turning into May.
My friend Ray has moved away.
I am feeling sad today.
I grow older on this day.
It's my birthday. Shout hooray!

This rhyme includes words your child is working with in school: words with the long *a* sound spelled *a, ai,* and *ay* (*changes, rain, may*) and verbs that end in *-s, -es,* and *-ing* (*turns, changes, feeling*). Sing "Changes" with your child, raising your hands each time a long *a* word is sung.

(fold here)

Name: _____

You are your child's first and best teacher!

Here are ways to help your child practice skills while having fun!

Day 1 Write several simple sentences containing verbs that end with *-s, -es,* or *-ing,* such as *takes, pushes, falling.* Help your child read each sentence and draw a picture for it.

Day 2 Write the words *keep, mother, myself, new,* and *warm* on index cards. Take turns drawing two cards at a time. Try using both words in one sentence.

Day 3 Find two pictures of two different settings, such as New York City and Yosemite National Park. Challenge your child to think of how the places are alike and different.

Day 4 Make up sentences and leave blanks where the nouns would be. Have your child suggest nouns, silly or serious, that might be used in their places. *A dog drove the car!*

Day 5 Your child is learning to give directions. Ask him or her to give directions for doing something interesting, such as teaching a dog a new trick.

Read with your child EVERY DAY!

Long a Rhymes

Materials 1 button per player

Game Directions

1. Players take turns tossing buttons on the gameboard and saying as many words as possible that rhyme with the word landed on.

2. Players earn 1 point for each rhyming word said. The first player to get 15 points wins!

rain	cake
pail	hay
play	face
frame	mail

Name _____

Read each sentence.
Circle the word with the **long a** sound.
Write the word on the line.

n<u>ai</u>l

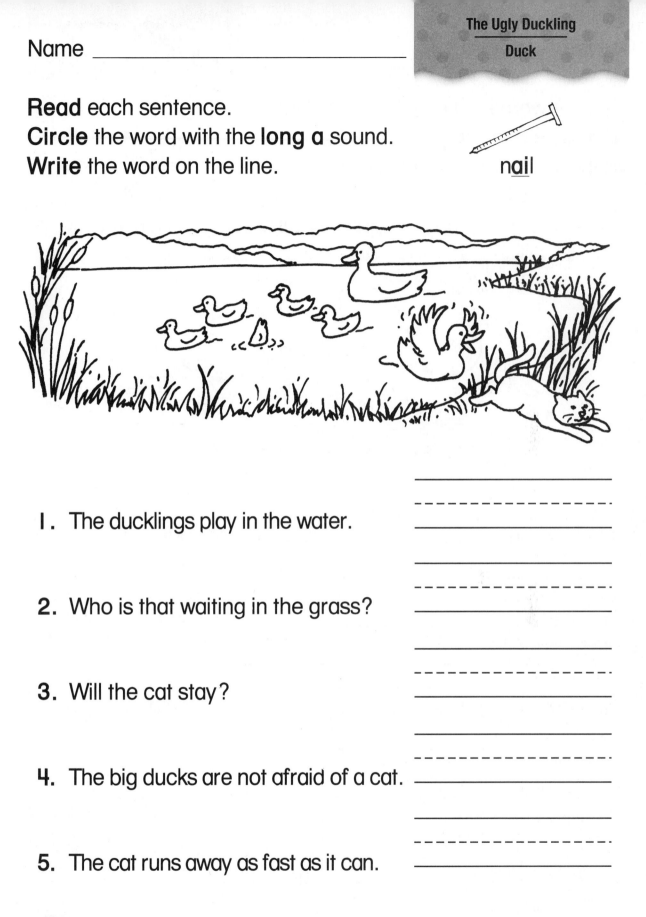

1. The ducklings play in the water.

_____
- - - - - - - - - - - - - - - -

2. Who is that waiting in the grass?

_____
- - - - - - - - - - - - - - - -

3. Will the cat stay?

_____
- - - - - - - - - - - - - - - -

4. The big ducks are not afraid of a cat.

_____
- - - - - - - - - - - - - - - -

5. The cat runs away as fast as it can.

_____
- - - - - - - - - - - - - - - -

Notes for Home: Your child identified words in which the long *a* sound is spelled *ai* or *ay* (*nail, play*). **Home Activity:** Have your child read and "collect" sentences with long *a* words. Together, draw a picture illustrating each sentence.

Name _____

Use the word in ( ) to finish each sentence.
Add -s, -es, or **-ing** to the word.
Write the new word on the line.

Ben shop**s**.   He push**es** a cart.   Ben is walk**ing**.

1. The hen _____ on her eggs. (sit)

2. She _____ "chirp, chirp, chirp." (hear)

3. Now one egg _____ . (hatch)

4. A chick _____ its way out. (push)

5. It is _____ up. (stand)

Notes for Home: Your child added *-s, -es,* and *-ing* to verbs—words that show action *(shops, pushes, walking)*. **Home Activity:** Create sentences for your child like those above. Ask your child whether he or she would add *-s, -es,* or *-ing* to the verb to finish each sentence.

© Scott Foresman 2

Name _____

Pick a word from the box to finish each sentence.
Write the word on the line. Use each word only once.

| keep | mother | myself | new | warm |

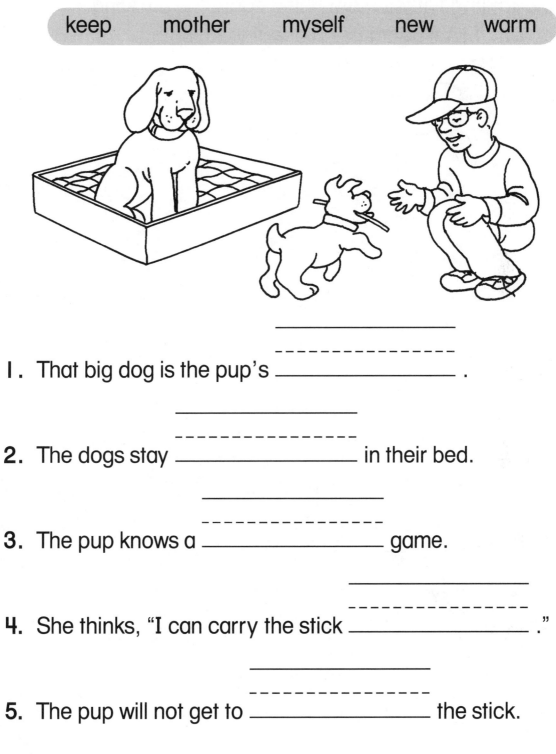

1. That big dog is the pup's _____ .

2. The dogs stay _____ in their bed.

3. The pup knows a _____ game.

4. She thinks, "I can carry the stick _____ ."

5. The pup will not get to _____ the stick.

Notes for Home: This week your child is learning to read the words *keep, mother, myself, new,* and *warm. Home Activity:* Help your child use these words to write about a baby animal that he or she has seen.

Name _____

Read the words.
Write duck if it tells something about the duck.
Write duckling if it tells something about the duckling.
Write both if it tells something about them both.

duck

duckling

I. beak _____

2. big _____

3. little _____

4. fuzzy down _____

5. webbed feet _____

Notes for Home: Your child identified the ways in which two things are alike and different.
Home Activity: Point out two household objects that have something in common, such as a
lamp and a flashlight. Ask your child to tell how they are alike and how they are different.

Name _____

Butterball Duck	Swan
It is small.	It is large.
It makes nests in hollow trees.	It makes big nests of grass and twigs beside the water.
It lays 10-12 eggs.	It lays 4-5 eggs.
It eats mostly small sea animals.	It eats mostly plants.

Use facts from the table to answer each question.
Circle or **write** the answer.

1. Which bird is bigger?   Butterball Duck   Swan

2. Where do Butterball Ducks make their nests?

   _____

   _____

3. What do swans use to make their nests?

   _____

   _____

4. Which bird lays more eggs?   Butterball Duck   Swan

5. Which bird eats mostly plants?   Butterball Duck   Swan

Notes for Home: Your child answered questions based on information in a table. *Home Activity:* Have your child make a table to record and compare facts about two animals. Think about the size, color, sound, and diet of each animal.

© Scott Foresman 2

daisy

he

Circle the word with the **long e** sound.

1. muddy   pen

2. we   men

3. my   me

4. hurry   race

5. puppy   pet

6. write   study

7. baby   nest

8. penny   cent

Find the word that has the same **long e** sound as the picture.
Mark the space to show your answer.

9. ⬭ egg
   ⬭ be
   ⬭ blue

10. ⬭ ugly
    ⬭ cry
    ⬭ play

Notes for Home: Your child reviewed words with the long *e* sound spelled *y* and *e* (*daisy* and *he*). **Home Activity:** Have your child look through a story and find words that end in *y*. Discuss whether the *y* in each word stands for the long *e* sound.

Name _____

Part 1: Vocabulary

Find the word that best fits in each sentence.
Mark the space for your answer.

1. The duck eats with its _____ .
   ⬭ beak   ⬭ surface   ⬭ house

2. You can _____ that hat.
   ⬭ paddle   ⬭ explore   ⬭ keep

3. I can read that book _____ .
   ⬭ around   ⬭ myself   ⬭ many

4. The ducks _____ through the water.
   ⬭ paddle   ⬭ fix   ⬭ farm

5. Bugs land on the _____ of the water.
   ⬭ warm   ⬭ surface   ⬭ tool

© Scott Foresman 2

GO ON

Part 2: Comprehension

Read each question.
Mark the space for your answer.

6. The mother duck sits on her eggs to —
   - ⬭ hide them.
   - ⬭ lay them.
   - ⬭ keep them warm.

7. When can the duckling walk?
   - ⬭ when it is two days old
   - ⬭ as soon as it hatches
   - ⬭ when it is one week old

8. How is a six-week-old duckling different from a one-week-old duckling?
   - ⬭ It has webbed feet.
   - ⬭ It has a beak.
   - ⬭ It has white feathers.

9. Ducklings get food from —
   - ⬭ the mother duck.
   - ⬭ the water.
   - ⬭ yellow down.

10. When the ducks grow up, what will they do?
    - ⬭ talk
    - ⬭ read
    - ⬭ take care of ducklings

STOP

Pick the word that rhymes.
Write the word on the line.

hatch**ed**

I. pecked

nest   next   checked

- - - - - - - - - - - - - - -

2. rowed

toad   floated   slow

- - - - - - - - - - - - - - -

---

3. stayed

play   made   waited

- - - - - - - - - - - - - - -

4. nested

west   dressed   rested

- - - - - - - - - - - - - - -

---

5. smelled

melt   held   helped

- - - - - - - - - - - - - - -

6. missed

fizz   list   sled

- - - - - - - - - - - - - - -

Find the word that has the same ending sound as **lost**.
Mark the space to show your answer.

7. ⬭ moss
   ⬭ tossed
   ⬭ posted

8. ⬭ crossed
   ⬭ tested
   ⬭ close

Notes for Home: Your child reviewed words that end in *-ed*. **Home Activity:** Point out words like these when you read with your child. Help your child say these words aloud. Discuss the different ways that words ending in *-ed* can sound as in *played, rested,* or *missed.*

| passes | passing | teaches | teaching | wishes | wishing |

Change one or two letters in each word to make a word from the box.

Write the new word on the line.

1. dishes

_____

- - - - - - - - - - - - - - - - -

_____

2. beaches

_____

- - - - - - - - - - - - - - - - -

_____

3. passed

_____

- - - - - - - - - - - - - - - - -

_____

4. fishing

_____

- - - - - - - - - - - - - - - - -

_____

5. reaching

_____

- - - - - - - - - - - - - - - - -

_____

6. tossing

_____

- - - - - - - - - - - - - - - - -

_____

Pick a word from the box to finish each sentence.
Write the word on the line.

mother
myself

_____

- - - - - - - - - - - - - - - -

7. My _____ is teaching me to swim.

_____

- - - - - - - - - - - - - - - -

8. Soon I will swim by _____ .

Notes for Home: Your child spelled words ending in *-es* or *-ing*, such as *passes* and *passing*, and two frequently used words: *mother, myself.* **Home Activity:** Help your child think of and spell words that rhyme with some of the spelling words on this page.

© Scott Foresman 2

Eye Spy

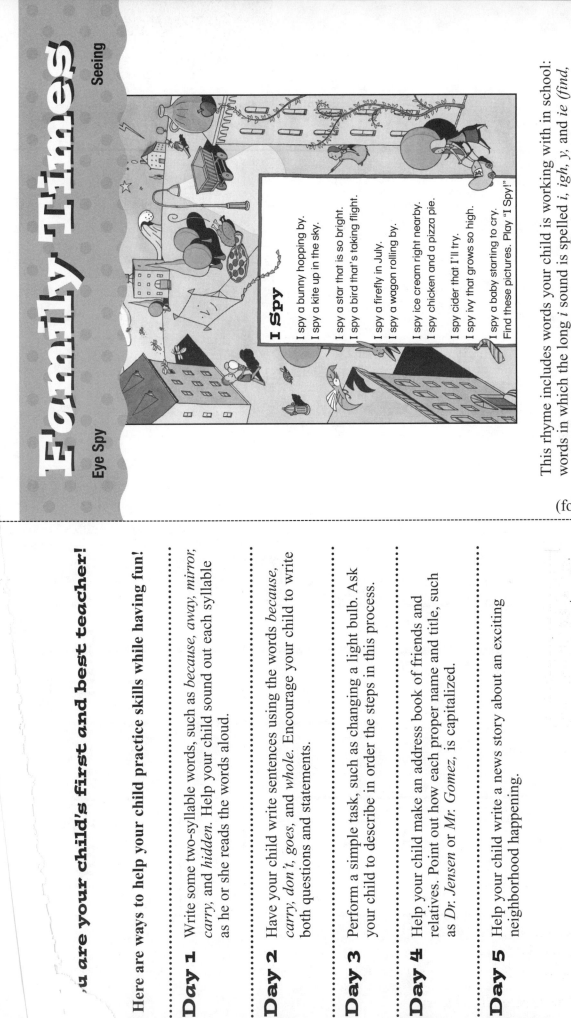

I Spy

I spy a bunny hopping by.
I spy a kite up in the sky.

I spy a star that is so bright.
I spy a bird that's taking flight.

I spy a firefly in July.
I spy a wagon rolling by.

I spy ice cream right nearby.
I spy chicken and a pizza pie.

I spy cider that I'll try.
I spy ivy that grows so high.

I spy a baby starting to cry.
Find these pictures. Play "I Spy!"

This rhyme includes words your child is working with in school: words in which the long *i* sound is spelled *i*, *igh*, *y*, and *ie* (*find, high, sky, pie*) and two-syllable words (*bunny, baby*). After saying the rhyme, play "I Spy." Offer clues to items in the room with the long *i* sound for your child to guess.

(fold here)

Name: _____

---

u are your child's first and best teacher!

Here are ways to help your child practice skills while having fun!

Day 1 Write some two-syllable words, such as *because, away, mirror, carry,* and *hidden.* Help your child sound out each syllable as he or she reads the words aloud.

Day 2 Have your child write sentences using the words *because, carry, don't, goes,* and *whole.* Encourage your child to write both questions and statements.

Day 3 Perform a simple task, such as changing a light bulb. Ask your child to describe in order the steps in this process.

Day 4 Help your child make an address book of friends and relatives. Point out how each proper name and title, such as *Dr. Jensen* or *Mr. Gomez,* is capitalized.

Day 5 Help your child write a news story about an exciting neighborhood happening.

Read with your child EVERY DAY!

Spin a Word

Materials   paper, paper clip, pencil,
1 button per player

Game Directions

1. Make a simple spinner as shown.

2. Place buttons on Start and take turns spinning the spinner.

3. If the word ending shown on the spinner can be combined with the letter or letters on the next gameboard space to make a word, player moves button to that space.

4. The first player to reach the end wins!

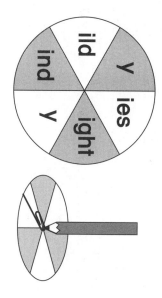

y	ies
ild	ight
ind	y

Start
s
cr
fl
l
m
f
tr
End

Start
dr
n
r
wh
sk
fr
sh
End

Name _____

Circle a word to finish each sentence.   sky   night   tie

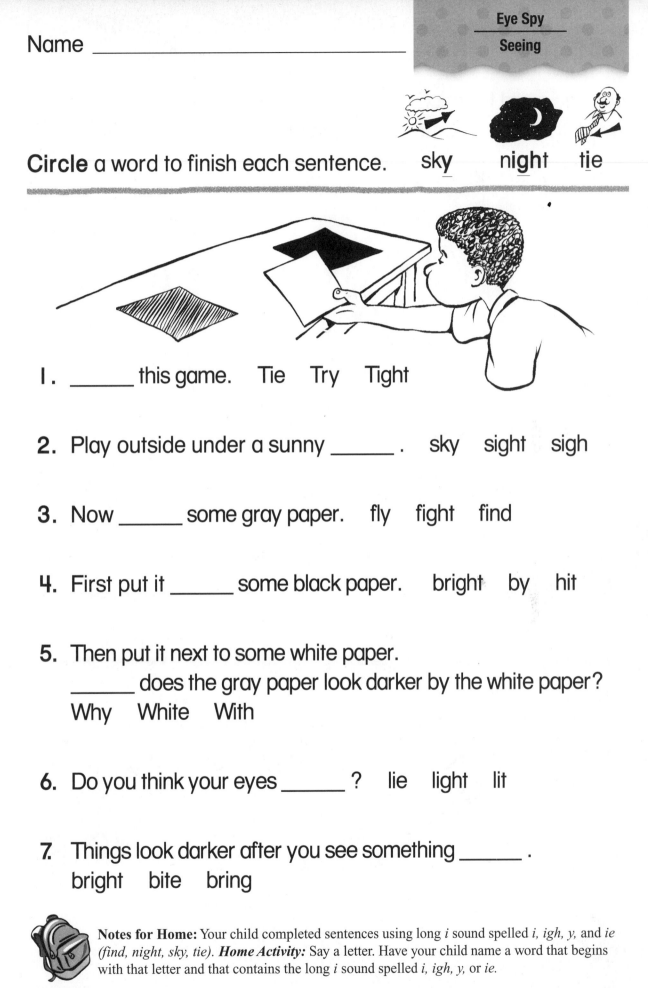

1. _____ this game.   Tie   Try   Tight

2. Play outside under a sunny _____ .   sky   sight   sigh

3. Now _____ some gray paper.   fly   fight   find

4. First put it _____ some black paper.   bright   by   hit

5. Then put it next to some white paper.
   _____ does the gray paper look darker by the white paper?
   Why   White   With

6. Do you think your eyes _____ ?   lie   light   lit

7. Things look darker after you see something _____ .
   bright   bite   bring

Notes for Home: Your child completed sentences using long *i* sound spelled *i, igh, y,* and *ie* (*find, night, sky, tie*). **Home Activity:** Say a letter. Have your child name a word that begins with that letter and that contains the long *i* sound spelled *i, igh, y,* or *ie.*

Name _____

Say the word for each picture.
Write the letter or letters from the box to finish each word.

| g | l | nd | pp | rr |

stu<u>d</u>ent

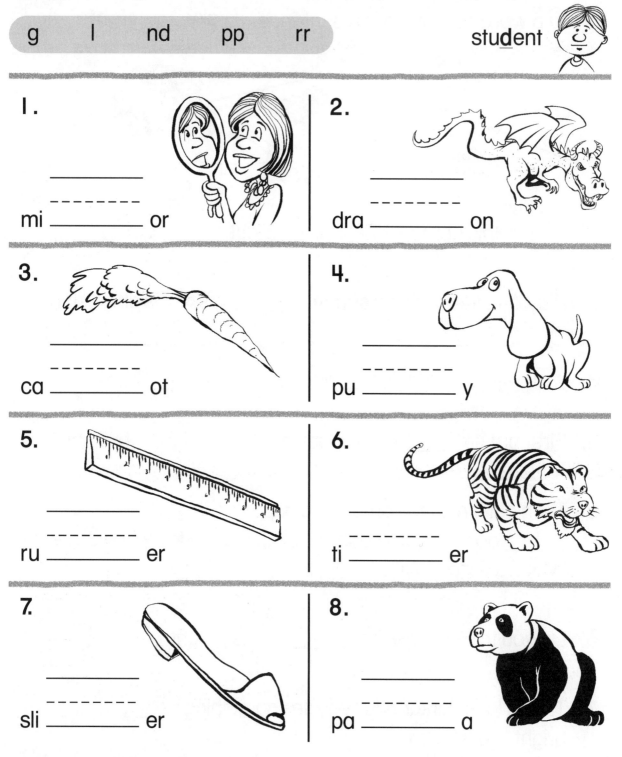

1.

_____
- - - - - -
mi _____ or

2.

_____
- - - - - -
dra _____ on

3.

_____
- - - - - -
ca _____ ot

4.

_____
- - - - - -
pu _____ y

5.

_____
- - - - - -
ru _____ er

6.

_____
- - - - - -
ti _____ er

7.

_____
- - - - - -
sli _____ er

8.

_____
- - - - - -
pa _____ a

Notes for Home: Your child wrote the missing middle consonants for two-syllable words.
Home Activity: Write and draw pictures of a few two-syllable words, such as *letter, camel,* and *napkin.* Help your child sound out and read each word.

Pick a word from the box to finish each sentence.
Write the word on the line.

| because | carry | don't | goes | whole |

1. The boy _____ to get the melon.

2. Can he _____ it?

3. I _____ think he can.

4. The _____ melon is too big.

5. He can carry a slice _____ it is small.

Notes for Home: This week your child is learning to read the words *because, carry, don't, goes,* and *whole.* **Home Activity:** Encourage your child to write an explanation of how some simple machine works, using as many of these words as possible.

Name _____

Look at the pictures. **Read** the steps.
Write a number from **I to 5** to show the right order.
One is done for you.

- - - - -   Tie strings through the holes.

_____   First, draw a big bowl on one side of
- - - - -   a card.
_____

_____   Last, use your thumbs and fingers
- - - - -   to make the card spin fast.
_____   You will see a fish in a bowl!

---

3   Make a hole on one side of the card
_____   and then the other.

_____   Next, draw a fish on the other side of
- - - - -   the card.
_____

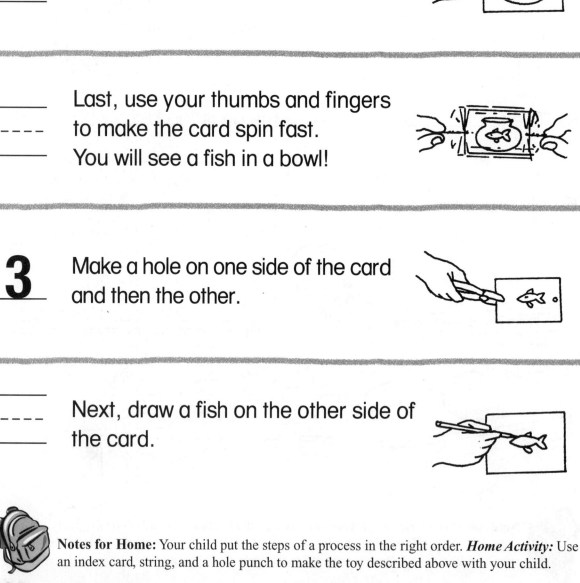

© Scott Foresman 2

Name _____

lady   mail   May

Circle the word with the **long a** sound.

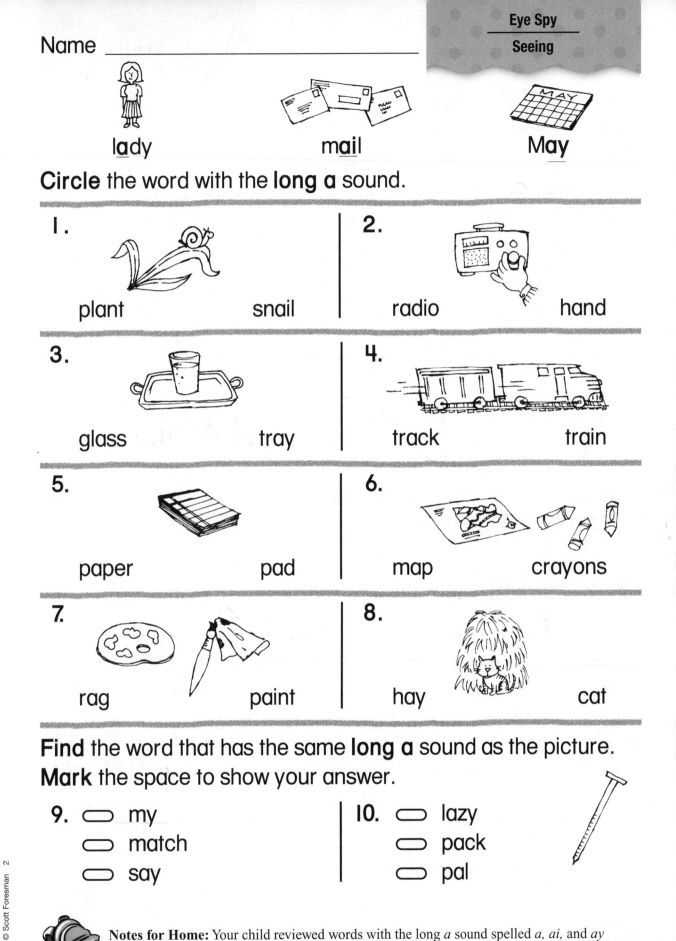

1. plant   snail

2. radio   hand

3. glass   tray

4. track   train

5. paper   pad

6. map   crayons

7. rag   paint

8. hay   cat

Find the word that has the same **long a** sound as the picture.
Mark the space to show your answer.

9. ◯ my
   ◯ match
   ◯ say

10. ◯ lazy
    ◯ pack
    ◯ pal

Notes for Home: Your child reviewed words with the long *a* sound spelled *a, ai,* and *ay* as in *lady, mail,* and *May.* **Home Activity:** Have your child look through store ads and circle words in which the long *a* sound is spelled *a, ai,* or *ay.*

Name _____

| bright | sight | line | side | sky | try |

Read the word at the top of each column.
Pick a word from the box that has the same spelling for the **long i** sound.
Write the word on the line.

why

smile

high

1. _____

3. _____

5. _____

2. _____

4. _____

6. _____

Pick a word from the box to match each clue.
Write the word on the line.

7. You see stars up there.

_____

8. star light, star _____

_____

Pick a word from the box to finish each sentence.
Write it on the line.

because
whole

9. I ate the _____ thing!

10. That's _____ it was so good!

Notes for Home: Your child spelled words with the long *i* sound spelled *igh, y,* and *i-consonant-e* as in *bright, try,* and *line* and two frequently used words: *because, whole.*
Home Activity: Have your child use the spelling words to write about looking at the stars.

108 Spelling: Long *i: igh, y, i-e*

Level 2.1

© Scott Foresman 2

Part 1: Vocabulary

Find the word that best fits in each sentence.
Mark the space for your answer.

1. You use your _____ to think.
   ⬭ beak   ⬭ brain   ⬭ thumb

2. Alex took two _____ for his dad.
   ⬭ messages   ⬭ world   ⬭ surface

3. I can see you in the _____ .
   ⬭ tomorrow   ⬭ hidden   ⬭ mirror

4. You have one _____ on each hand.
   ⬭ thumb   ⬭ time   ⬭ beak

5. My sister ate the _____ cake!
   ⬭ surprised   ⬭ whole   ⬭ pleased

GO ON ▶

Part 2: Comprehension

Read each question.
Mark the space for your answer.

6. Your pupils let in just the right amount of light by changing —
   - ⬭ size.
   - ⬭ shape.
   - ⬭ color.

7. What happens first as the eye sees?
   - ⬭ Messages go to the brain.
   - ⬭ Light goes into the eye.
   - ⬭ A picture is made at the back of the eyeball.

8. Which of these did you find out from reading?
   - ⬭ Your eyeball is not really a ball.
   - ⬭ People who are far away are smaller.
   - ⬭ Your brain tries to make sense of what you see.

9. Which is a good title for this story?
   - ⬭ "Two Dogs in a Vase"
   - ⬭ "How Your Eyes Work"
   - ⬭ "Why Some Eyes Are Blue"

10. Which sentence is true?
    - ⬭ You need your brain and your eyes to see.
    - ⬭ Light goes into your brain.
    - ⬭ A friend is smaller than a thumb.

pitch**es**

play**ing**

hit**s**

Read each sentence.
Circle the verb that makes sense in the sentence.

1. Dad _____ the show.   watches   watching

2. Sam _____ off his hat.   pulls   pulling

3. Kay _____ a rabbit in the hat.   puts   putting

4. Sam is _____ the hat with a wand.   taps   tapping

5. Sam is _____ a skunk out of the hat! takes   taking

Find the word that makes sense in the sentences below.
Mark the space to show your answer.

Sam _____ his cape. | He _____ it over the hat.

6. ⬭ flings | 7. ⬭ tossing
   ⬭ flinging | ⬭ toss
   ⬭ fling | ⬭ tosses

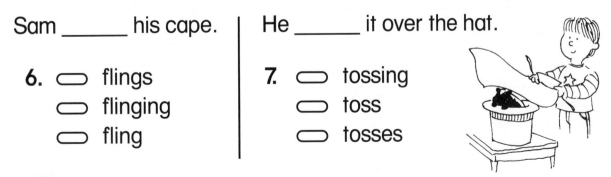

Notes for Home: Your child reviewed verbs with *-s, -es,* and *-ing* endings. **Home Activity:** Read with your child, looking for sentences with verbs ending in *-ing.* (*He is washing the dog.*) Have your child write the sentence using another form of the verb. (*He washes the dog.*)

bright   sight   line   side   sky   try

Change one letter in each word to make a word from the box.
Write the word on the line.

1. ride

_____

- - - - - - - - - - - - -

_____

2. fine

_____

- - - - - - - - - - - -

_____

Write two words that rhyme with [image] .

_____

- - - - - - - - - - - -

3. _____

_____

- - - - - - - - - - - -

4. _____

Write two words from the box that rhyme with **cry**.

_____

- - - - - - - - - - - -

5. _____

_____

- - - - - - - - - - - -

6. _____

because   whole

Write the word from the box that fits in each puzzle.

7.

8.

Notes for Home: Your child spelled words with the long *i* sound spelled *igh, y,* and *i-consonant-e (bright, try,* and *line)* and two frequently used words: *because, whole.* **Home Activity:** Have your child sort the long *i* words according to their long *i* spellings.

Family Times

Furry Mouse

Two Mice

What a Perky Group!

It's party time for turtles
And birds and turkeys too.
The perky turkeys serve the food.
They've made a tasty stew.

Bert the bird stirs the stew
And perches on his swing.
When he's done he turns around
And chirps and twirls his wing.

The turtle babies drink some milk
And serve themselves some soup.
They whirl around and laugh a lot.
What a perky group!

This rhyme includes words your child is working with in school: words with *er, ir,* and *ur (serve, stirs, turtles)* and nouns that name more than one *(birds, babies)*. Say the words to "What a Perky Group!" together. Then find all the words that have the same vowel sound heard in *perky* spelled *er, ir,* and *ur.*

(fold here)

1

Name: _____

You are your child's first and best teacher!

Here are ways to help your child practice skills while having fun!

Day 1 Listen to the vowel sound in *her, first,* and *turn.* Together, make up lists of words with that same vowel sound spelled *er, ir,* and *ur (fern, bird, hurt).*

Day 2 Tell your child to hide an object. Then ask him or her to give you one clue at a time to help you find the object, using these words: *almost, another, around, food,* and *under.*

Day 3 Pick a simple object for you and your child to draw. Draw separate pictures. When done, have your child tell what is alike and different in the pictures you both drew.

Day 4 Read some poems with your child. Listen for words that repeat, rhyme, or represent interesting sounds.

Day 5 Help your child write a list of the contents of a kitchen or refrigerator shelf using singular nouns *(can)* and plural nouns *(boxes).*

Read with your child EVERY DAY!

4

Toss for Two

Materials paper, markers, scissors, bag, tape, 2 small bowls, 12 buttons per player

Game Directions

1. Copy and cut out the words shown on page 3. Put the words in a bag. Copy and cut out the word endings below. Tape one word ending to each bowl. Place the bowls on the floor.

2. Players take turns drawing a word from the bag and tossing a button into the bowl labeled with the plural ending for that word, such as -es for cherries.

3. If the button lands in the right bowl, the player spells the plural word and gets 1 point.

4. The player with the most points when the bag is empty wins!

Word Endings

-s   -es

cherry	city	jelly
baby	berry	pony
star	wheel	turkey
bug	acorn	cub
story	kitty	penny
party	monkey	toy
ant	dog	song
light	feather	friend

3

Say each word.
Circle 7 words that have the same vowel sound as **shirt**.
Write these words on the lines.

sh<u>ir</u>t

---

1. her
_____
- - - - - - - - - - -
_____

2. surf
_____
- - - - - - - - - - -
_____

---

3. stir
_____
- - - - - - - - - - -
_____

4. bird
_____
- - - - - - - - - - -
_____

---

5. warm
_____
- - - - - - - - - - -
_____

6. herd
_____
- - - - - - - - - - -
_____

---

7. fur
_____
- - - - - - - - - - -
_____

8. start
_____
- - - - - - - - - - -
_____

---

9. wore
_____
- - - - - - - - - - -
_____

10. perch
_____
- - - - - - - - - - -
_____

Notes for Home: Your child identified words that contain the vowel sound in *shirt*.
Home Activity: Think of a letter. Challenge your child to name a word that begins with that
letter and that has the same vowel sound as *shirt* spelled *er, ir,* or *ur.*

Name _____

cat**s**   box**es**   bab**ies**

Underline the sentence that matches each picture.

1. Look at the fat strawberry!

   Look at the fat strawberries!

2. Will the big bug eat the bush?

   Will the big bugs eat the bush?

3. Don't step on the snake.

   Don't step on the snakes.

4. Someone must water the rosebush.

   Someone must water the rosebushes.

Write a word to finish the sentence.

5. I see two _____ .

Notes for Home: Your child read the plural forms of nouns such as *cats, boxes,* and *babies.* **Home Activity:** Have your child read aloud to you. Listen to be sure your child is pronouncing the *-s* or *-es* sounds of the plurals. Ask: *Is that one or more than one?*

© Scott Foresman 2

Name _____

Pick a word from the box to finish each sentence.
Write the word on the line.

almost	another	around	food	under

1. The cub _____ fell.

2. He hides _____ a log.

3. He sees _____ cub.

4. They run _____ the tree.

5. They eat fish for _____ .

Notes for Home: This week your child is learning to read the words *almost, another, around, food,* and *under.* **Home Activity:** Watch a wildlife show or look at a wildlife book with your child. Have your child use some of these words to write about what he or she saw.

Name _____

jay   canary

Look for ways in which the jay bird is **not** like the canary.
Write two sentences about the jay bird.

1. _____

2. _____

Write one sentence that tells how both birds are alike.

3. _____

Look for ways in which the canary is **not** like the jay bird.
Write two sentences about the canary.

4. _____

5. _____

Notes for Home: Your child described ways in which two things are alike and different.
Home Activity: Talk with your child about members of your own family. Encourage your child
to identify ways two or more people are alike and different.

© Scott Foresman 2

Name _____

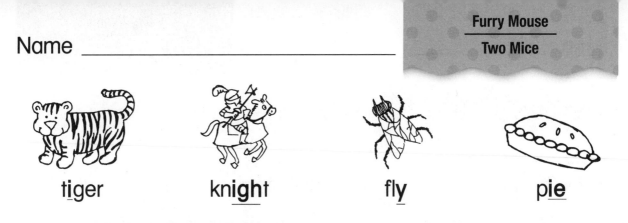

tiger   kn**igh**t   fl**y**   p**ie**

Circle the word for each picture.

1. night   neat

2. fry   free

3. spice   spider

4. type   tip

5. lean   lion

6. fling   flight

7. tie   tin

8. list   light

Find the word that has the same **long i** sound as the picture.
Mark the space to show your answer.

9. ⬭ lie
    ⬭ lip
    ⬭ lay

10. ⬭ slip
    ⬭ she
    ⬭ shy

Notes for Home: Your child reviewed the long *i* sound spelled *i, igh, y,* and *ie.* **Home Activity:** Help your child write a story using some of the words on this page, as well as some of these words: *pilot, bicycle, mind, wild, night, fright, sight, sky, try,* and *my.*

Name _____

baby   babies   bunny   bunnies   friend   friends

Read the words above each column.
Write the words from the box in the correct column.

Names One	Names More Than One
1. _____	2. _____
3. _____	4. _____
5. _____	6. _____

Pick a word from the box to match each clue.
Write the word on the line.

7. one pal

_____

8.   two rabbits

_____

Pick a word from the box to finish each sentence.
Write the word on the line.

another   food

9. Carrots are _____ that bunnies like to eat.

10. They will always eat _____ carrot.

Notes for Home: Your child spelled singular and plural nouns, such as *baby* and *babies,* and two frequently used words: *another, food.* **Home Activity:** Help your child make a list of his or her favorite things. Some of the words on the list should be singular, and others plural.

Look at the picture.
Circle the word next to the picture if you see just one.
Write a plural word if you see more than one.

1. bunny

2. bus

3. dish

4. cherry

5. wheel

6. light

7. boy

8. box

9. egg

10. brush

Notes for Home: Your child identified singular and plural nouns. *Home Activity:* Help your child make a list of the objects in a refrigerator, closet, or drawer. Discuss which plural nouns end in -*s* and which end in -*es*.

Test-Taking Tips

1. Write your name on the test.

2. Read each question twice.

3. Read all the answer choices for the question.

4. Mark your answer carefully.

5. Check your answer.

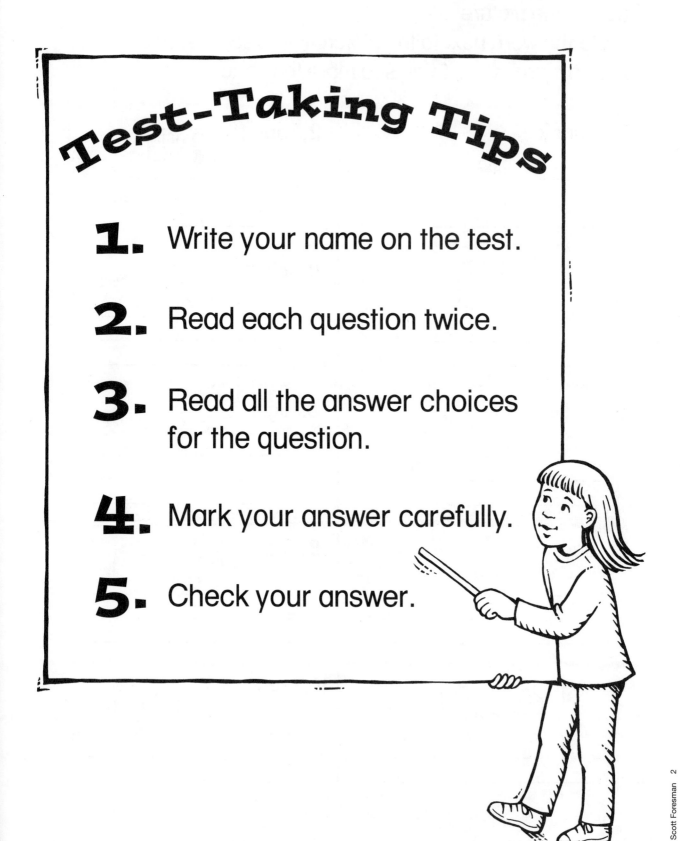

© Scott Foresman 2

Part 1: Vocabulary

Find the word that best fits in each sentence.
Mark the space for your answer.

1. Jen has a cat, but she wants _____ one.
   - ⬭ everywhere
   - ⬭ many
   - ⬭ another

2. The baby drinks from a _____ .
   - ⬭ spider
   - ⬭ bottle
   - ⬭ house

3. The cat will _____ the mouse.
   - ⬭ write
   - ⬭ paddle
   - ⬭ follow

4. The dog's _____ comes in a can.
   - ⬭ food
   - ⬭ wheel
   - ⬭ brain

5. My bird lives in a _____ .
   - ⬭ bottle
   - ⬭ cage
   - ⬭ beak

GO ON ▶

Name _____

Part 2: Comprehension

Read each question.
Mark the space for your answer.

6. In this story, the inside mouse eats —
   - ⬭ food from a bowl.
   - ⬭ rose leaves.
   - ⬭ strawberries and acorns.

7. Who almost ate the two mice?
   - ⬭ a dog
   - ⬭ a snake
   - ⬭ a cat

8. How is the outside mouse different from the inside mouse?
   - ⬭ He takes many naps.
   - ⬭ He lives in a cage.
   - ⬭ He likes to run around a lot.

9. After going out, the inside mouse was ready to —
   - ⬭ take a nap.
   - ⬭ run on the wheel.
   - ⬭ eat acorns.

10. The inside mouse probably thinks that —
    - ⬭ raccoons are friendly.
    - ⬭ outside is not a very safe place.
    - ⬭ the outside mouse wants to move inside.

Name _____

monkey   rabbit   ti**g**er

| b | ct | g | ll | lr | rr | sk | tt |

Pick a letter or a pair of letters from the box.
Write the letter or pair of letters to finish each word.

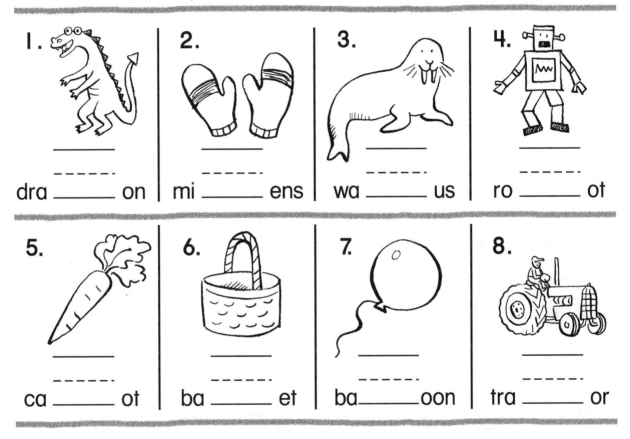

1. dra _____ on

2. mi _____ ens

3. wa _____ us

4. ro _____ ot

5. ca _____ ot

6. ba _____ et

7. ba _____ oon

8. tra _____ or

Find the word with the same middle consonant sound as .
Mark the space to show your answer.

9. ⬭ muffin
   ⬭ kitten
   ⬭ paper

10. ⬭ butter
    ⬭ wagon
    ⬭ ruler

Notes for Home: Your child reviewed words with more than one syllable that have one or two consonants in the middle, such as *tiger, monkey* and *rabbit*. **Home Activity:** Together, draw and label pictures of each word above. Practice reading these words aloud.

© Scott Foresman 2

Level 2.1   **Phonics: Medial Consonants Review** **129** baby   babies   bunny   bunnies   friend   friends

Pick a word from the box to finish the math sentence.
Write the word on the line.

1. 👤 + 👶 = 2 _____

2. 👧 + 👦 = 2 _____

3. 🐰 + 🐰🐰 = 3 _____

4. 🐰🐰🐰 – 🐰🐰 = 1 _____

Write the word from the box that rhymes with each word below.

5. bend

_____

6. maybe

_____

Pick a word from the box to match each clue.
Write the word on the line.

another   food

7. something to eat

_____

8. one more

_____

Notes for Home: Your child spelled singular and plural nouns *(baby* and *babies)* and two frequently used words: *another, food.* **Home Activity:** Have your child draw and label pictures of these words: *ponies, dog, snakes,* and *zebra.*

Family Times

Snakes

The Old Gollywampus

Moe and Joe

Outside by my treehouse,
Lives Moe the old toad.
Moe croaks in the nighttime.
Moe roams by a road.

Inside my own bedroom,
Lives my goldfish, Joe.
Joe likes his new fishbowl.
Oh, Joe told me so.

When it is midnight,
We don't hear a peep.
Then Moe starts his croaking.
We can't go to sleep.

This rhyme includes words your child is working with in school: words with the long *o* sound spelled *o, oa, ow,* and *oe* (*old, toad, fishbowl, Moe*) and compound words made up of two smaller words (*outside*). Say the rhyme together, stomping your foot for each long *o* word.

(fold here)

Name: _____

You are your child's first and best teacher!

Here are ways to help your child practice skills while having fun!

Day 1 Set a timer for 2 minutes and ask your child to list words that have the long *o* sound spelled *o, oa, ow,* and *oe,* such as *go, soap, grow,* and *toe.*

Day 2 Write these five words on index cards: *animals, before, between, knew,* and *why.* Take turns picking a word and using it in a sentence. Try to make the five sentences tell a story.

Day 3 Your child is learning to read and create charts, tables, graphs, and maps. Work with your child to create a simple map that shows the route your child takes to school.

Day 4 Find a photograph that shows your family having fun. Have your child make a short speech to you about the experience, referring to the photograph as he or she speaks.

Day 5 Write a general statement about an animal. (For example: *It is hard being a skunk.*) Have your child write sentences that give details to support the idea.

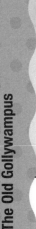

Read with your child EVERY DAY!

Combining Words

Materials 2 buttons per player, paper, pencil

Game Directions

1. Players take turns tossing buttons on the gameboard to try to make compound words.

2. Players earn 1 point for each compound word. Do not use a word more than once. Make a list to keep track of words used.

3. The first player to earn 10 points wins!

out	sun	time	shine
day	line	side	under
any	one	body	pop
every	where	corn	ground
coat	ball	rain	no
some	in	thing	base

Name _____

Circle the word in each row with the **long o** sound.
Write the word on the line.

b<u>ow</u>l

1. toad   top   two   _____

2. cop   cost   cold   _____

3. spoon   snow   soon   _____

4. out   over   one   _____

5. most   moss   mop   _____

6. took   toss   toast   _____

7. to   toe   too   _____

8. not   nod   know   _____

9. coat   cob   could   _____

10. pop   post   pots   _____

Notes for Home: Your child identified words in which the long *o* sound is spelled *o, oa, ow,* and *oe.* **Home Activity:** Write the word endings: *-oe, -oad, -oak, -oat, -old,* and *-ow,* on slips of paper. Have your child add beginning letters to each ending to form long *o* words.

Name _____

Use the pictures to make a compound word.
Write the compound word on the line.
Look at the words in the box if you need help.

cupcake   mailbox   raincoat
starfish   sunflower

rattlesnake

1.  ⭐ + 🐟 = _____

2.  ☔ + 🧥 = _____

3.  ☀ + 🌻 = _____

4.  ☕ + 🎂 = _____

5.  ✉ + 📦 = _____

Notes for Home: Your child formed compound words—words that are made up of two smaller words. *Home Activity:* Have fun with your child making up picture puzzles for other compound words, such as *toothbrush*.

Pick a word from the box to finish each sentence.
Write the word on the line.

| animals | before | between | knew | Why |

1. _____ did you jump back?

2. I saw some strange _____ .

3. They were _____ the rock and the dirt.

4. I _____ snakes lived under rocks.

5. But I've never seen one _____ !

Notes for Home: This week your child is learning to read the words *animals, before, between, knew,* and *why.* **Home Activity:** Read and discuss a book about reptiles with your child. Encourage your child to write a few sentences about the book, using some of these words.

Name _____

Read the table.
Answer the questions.

Animal	Things They Like to Eat
Birds	worms, bugs, berries, seeds
Bears	fish, berries
Rabbits	grass, plants, carrots
Sheep	grass
Spiders	bugs

1. Which animals like to eat bugs?

   _____

   -

   _____

2. Which animals like to eat berries?

   _____

   -

   _____

3. Which animals like to eat grass?

   _____

   -

   _____

4. Which animal likes to eat fish?

   _____

   -

   _____

 Notes for Home: Your child read a table and used information in it to answer questions. *Home Activity:* Help your child make a table that tells something about family members, such as favorite foods, songs, or colors.

Level 2.1

Name _____

fern   bird   surf

Circle the word for each picture.

1.	2.	3.	4.
turtle towel	short shirt	herd hard	hurt hut

5.	6.	7.	8.
dirt drift	nose nurse	desk dessert	clerk clock

Find the word that has the same vowel sound as the picture.
Mark the space to show your answer.

9. ○ trunk
    ○ first
    ○ near

10. ○ here
    ○ her
    ○ horse

Notes for Home: Your child reviewed words with *er, ir,* and *ur* that have the same vowel sound *(fern, bird,* and *surf). **Home Activity:** Use some of the following words to write sentences for your child to read aloud: *germ, herd, her, bird, chirp, dirt, burn, burst, purse.*

Name _____

| sold | woke | coat | soap | below | owe |

Write the word from the box that rhymes with each word below.

1. toe

_____

- - - - - - - - - - - - - -

_____

2. rope

_____

- - - - - - - - - - - - - -

_____

3. throat

_____

- - - - - - - - - - - - - -

_____

4. cold

_____

- - - - - - - - - - - - - -

_____

Pick a word from the box that is the opposite of each word below. Write the word on the line.

5. above

_____

- - - - - - - - - - - - - -

_____

6. slept

_____

- - - - - - - - - - - - - -

_____

Pick a word from the box to finish each sentence. Write the word on the line.

animals
between

_____

- - - - - - - - - - - - - -

7. Some _____ sleep when it is winter.

_____

- - - - - - - - - - - - - -

8. One sleeps _____ two rocks.

Notes for Home: Your child spelled words with the long *o* sound spelled *o, ow,* and *oa,* as well as two frequently used words: *animals, between.* **Home Activity:** Write simple sentences on slips of paper using these spelling words. Have your child read the sentences aloud.

140 Spelling: Long *o: o, oa, ow*

Level 2.1

© Scott Foresman 2

Part I: Vocabulary

Find the word that best fits in each sentence.
Mark the space for your answer.

1. We ran _____ the houses.
   ⬭ with   ⬭ between   ⬭ so

2. She _____ the banana.
   ⬭ peels   ⬭ follows   ⬭ fixes

3. This _____ will help you feel better.
   ⬭ enemy   ⬭ ground   ⬭ medicine

4. The snake's _____ are dry.
   ⬭ beaks   ⬭ messages   ⬭ scales

5. Ben found the ball _____ his bed.
   ⬭ there   ⬭ underneath   ⬭ after

GO ON ➡

Part 2: Comprehension
Read each question.
Mark the space for your answer.

6. Snakes have no —
   - ⬭ eyes.
   - ⬭ legs.
   - ⬭ scales.

7. Snakes use their tongues to —
   - ⬭ lick their food.
   - ⬭ pick up smells from the air.
   - ⬭ scare people.

8. Snakes "unhook" their jaws so they can —
   - ⬭ chew their food.
   - ⬭ clean their teeth.
   - ⬭ open their mouths wide.

9. To tell other animals to stay away, some snakes try to —
   - ⬭ run fast.
   - ⬭ look scary.
   - ⬭ sing songs.

10. Which sentence about snakes is true?
    - ⬭ Snakes sleep all winter.
    - ⬭ Snakes can see and hear very well.
    - ⬭ Snakes do not help people very much.

STOP

Name _____

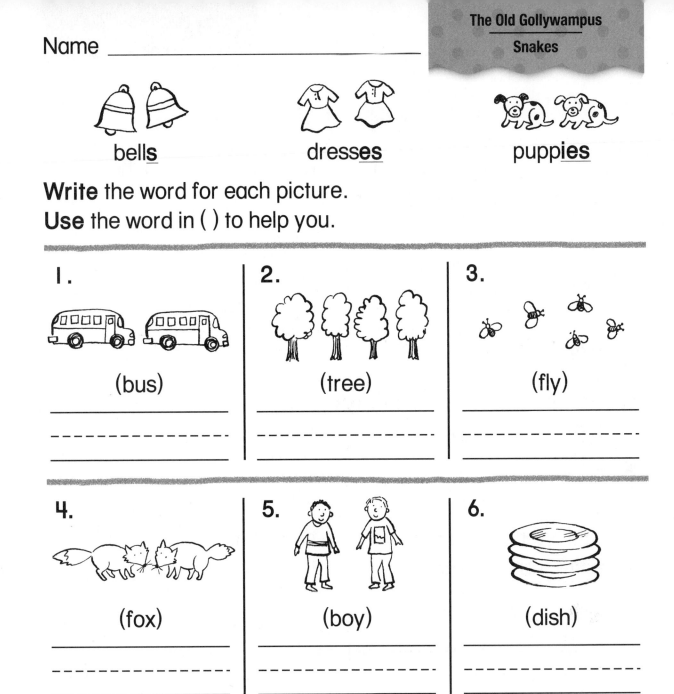

bell**s**   dress**es**   pupp**ies**

Write the word for each picture.
Use the word in ( ) to help you.

1.

(bus)

_____
_ _ _ _ _ _ _ _ _ _ _
_____

2.

(tree)

_____
_ _ _ _ _ _ _ _ _ _ _
_____

3.

(fly)

_____
_ _ _ _ _ _ _ _ _ _ _
_____

4.

(fox)

_____
_ _ _ _ _ _ _ _ _ _ _
_____

5.

(boy)

_____
_ _ _ _ _ _ _ _ _ _ _
_____

6.

(dish)

_____
_ _ _ _ _ _ _ _ _ _ _
_____

Find the word where you would add **-es** to show more than one.
Mark the space to show your answer.

7. ⬭ bush
   ⬭ book
   ⬭ bat

8. ⬭ girl
   ⬭ glass
   ⬭ gift

Notes for Home: Your child reviewed nouns that form plurals that end in *-s* and *-es*. **Home Activity:** Look in a catalog for pictures that show more than one thing, such as boxes. Help your child write the plural words to match these pictures.

Level 2.1

| sold | woke | coat | soap | below | owe |

Change one letter in each word to make a word from the box.
Write the new word on the line.

1. soak _____

2. wake _____

3. boat _____

4. cold _____

Write two words from the box with **ow**.

5. _____

6. _____

Pick a word from the box to match each clue.
Write the word on the line.

animals
between

7. in the middle
_____

8. lions, tigers, bears
_____

Notes for Home: Your child spelled words with the long *o* sound, spelled *o*, *oa*, and *ow*, as well as two frequently used words: *animals, between.* **Home Activity:** Help your child use some of these words to write rhymes. For example: *I put on my coat and got into the boat.*

Family Times

Spiders Up Close   Anansi and the Talking Melon

Horse's House

In Horse's house a spider hides
While mouse has Moose's Swiss cheese.
Moose is huge but the mouse is wise.
He steals the cheese with ease.

There's a mouse in Horse's house.
Mouse is such a big tease.
Spider watches Horse and Moose.
They want that piece of Swiss cheese!

This rhyme includes words your child is working with in school: words that end in *ce, ge,* and *se* (*piece, huge, horse, tease*) and words like *Horse's* that show possession. Sing "Horse's House" with your child as you march around a room.

(fold here)

Name: _____

You are your child's first and best teacher!

Here are ways to help your child practice skills while having fun!

Day 1   Take turns writing possessives using animals, such as *a spider's web, two monkeys' bananas,* and so on.

Day 2   Help your child to create a cartoon strip about a meal time. Have your child use the words *call, enough, full, heard,* and *until* to fill in the speech balloons.

Day 3   Find some newspaper cartoon strips that your child can read. Cut each strip apart and have your child arrange the panels in order.

Day 4   Your child is learning how to write a paragraph that clearly describes a person, place, or thing. Have your child write a short descriptive paragraph that describes a pet someone has lost.

Day 5   Encourage your child to describe several friends and classmates so that you can get a good mental picture of them.

Read with your child EVERY DAY!

How Many Words?

Materials   1 button, paper, pencils, timer

Game Directions

1. Take turns tossing the button on the gameboard.

2. All players have one minute to write as many words as possible that use the letters landed on. Players earn 1 point for each word. If another player has the same word, cross out the word and no points are earned.

3. The first player to earn 10 points wins!

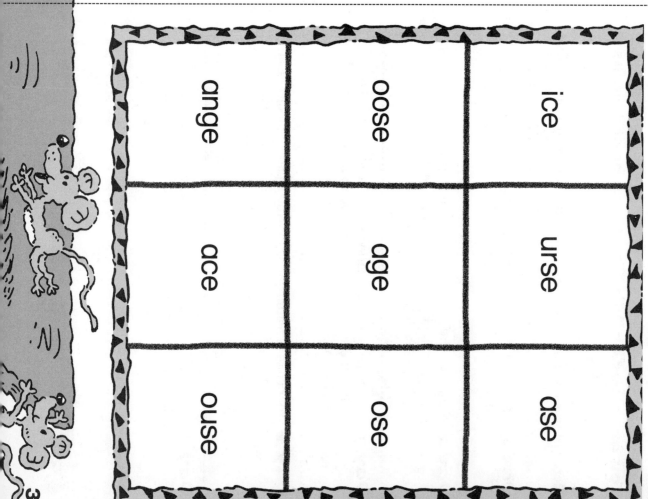

ice	urse	ase
oose	age	ose
ange	ace	ouse

2

3

Circle the word for each picture.

mi**ce**

1. mouth   mouse

2. cheese   cheap

3. ice   ink

4. cage   case

5. nice   nose

6. page   place

Draw a picture of each word.

7. house

8. face

Notes for Home: Your child practiced using words that end in *ce, ge,* and *se.* **Home Activity:** Give your child practice with words that end in *-ace, -ice, -uce, -aise, -ease, -eese, -ose, -ouse,* and words that end in *-ge,* such as *cage.* Take turns writing and reading rhyming pairs of these words.

Name _____

Circle the words that tell about each picture.

the **elephants'** trunks

1. the snake's hats
   the snakes' hats

2. the hog's slippers
   the hogs' slippers

3. the mice's game
   the mices' game

4. the fox's dinner
   the foxes' dinner

Draw a picture of the words below.

5. the mouse's cheese

Notes for Home: Your child identified possessives—words that show ownership.
Home Activity: Read a story with your child. Look for possessive forms of words.
Point them out and ask your child to tell you how many owners are being described.

Name _____

Pick a word from the box to finish each sentence.
Write the word on the line.

call	enough	full	heard	until

1. All day we _____ the king and queen yell.

2. They _____ out for more melons.

3. They can never eat _____ melons.

4. We picked melons _____ it was dark.

5. We hope they will be _____ soon.

Notes for Home: This week your child is learning to read the words *call, enough, full, heard,* and *until.* **Home Activity:** Help your child use these words to write a story about some talking animals. Encourage your child to read the story to others.

Look at the pictures. **Read** the sentences.
Write 1, 2, 3, 4 to show the right order.

a. Then, he picks up the box.

b. Next, he opens the box.

c. The monkey sees a box.

d. He takes the box home.

Write a sentence that tells what might happen next.

_____

_____

_____

Notes for Home: Your child figured out the order of events for a story. *Home Activity:* Have your child retell a favorite story. Listen to make sure that the story events are told in the correct order.

Name _____

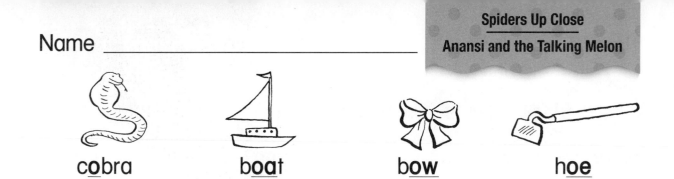

cobra   b**oa**t   b**ow**   h**oe**

Circle the word for each picture.

1.

cot   coat

2.

bowl   bull

3.

got   goat

4.

crow   cross

5.

soap   sap

6.

bat   boat

7.

toe   to

8.

tacks   tacos

Find the word that has the same long o sound as the picture. Mark the space to show your answer.

9. ⬭ food
⬭ fold
⬭ fox

10. ⬭ mop
⬭ moss
⬭ most

Notes for Home: Your child reviewed the long *o* sound heard in *cobra*, *boat*, *bow*, and *hoe*. *Home Activity:* Help your child cut out words with this sound and these spellings from a newspaper. Help him or her paste the words on paper and read them aloud.

| face | twice | cage | huge | page | tease |

Read the word at the top of each column.
Write the words from the box with the same ending sound.

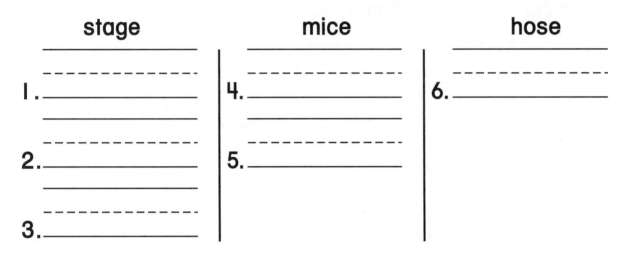

stage	mice	hose
1. _____	4. _____	6. _____
2. _____	5. _____	
3. _____		

Pick a word from the box to match each clue.
Write the word on the line.

7. very large

_____

8. two times

_____

Pick a word from the box to finish each sentence.
Write the word on the line.

| until |
| enough |

9. The king kept eating _____ it was dark.

10. He has had _____ !

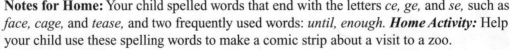

Notes for Home: Your child spelled words that end with the letters *ce*, *ge*, and *se*, such as *face*, *cage*, and *tease*, and two frequently used words: *until*, *enough*. **Home Activity:** Help your child use these spelling words to make a comic strip about a visit to a zoo.

Part 1: Vocabulary

Find the word that best fits in each sentence.
Mark the space for your answer.

1. Did you have _____ to eat?
   ⬭ never   ⬭ enough   ⬭ until

2. "Oh, no!" _____ Pat.
   ⬭ exclaimed   ⬭ surprised   ⬭ drew

3. Please don't walk on the _____ of new grass.
   ⬭ enemy   ⬭ mirror   ⬭ patch

4. You can eat melons when they are _____ .
   ⬭ ripe   ⬭ another   ⬭ later

5. Len could not _____ through the hole.
   ⬭ clean   ⬭ peel   ⬭ squeeze

GO ON ➡

Part 2: Comprehension

Read each question.
Mark the space for your answer.

6. What did Anansi use to make a hole in the melon?
   - ⬭ a rock
   - ⬭ a spoon
   - ⬭ a thorn

7. Anansi could not get out of the melon because —
   - ⬭ he was too fat from eating.
   - ⬭ the hole had gotten smaller.
   - ⬭ someone had covered the hole.

8. Which animal did Elephant see first?
   - ⬭ Warthog
   - ⬭ Hippo
   - ⬭ Ostrich

9. Why did the king get angry at the melon?
   - ⬭ The melon insulted him.
   - ⬭ The melon tasted bad.
   - ⬭ The melon would not talk to him.

10. Why will Elephant **not** take talking bananas to the king?
    - ⬭ He will want to keep the bananas for himself.
    - ⬭ He will want to share the bananas with Anansi.
    - ⬭ He will be afraid the bananas will get him in trouble.

Na___e _____

Say ___e word for each picture.
Use t___ words to make a compound
word th___ stands for the picture.
Write th___ compound word on the line.

wart + hog = warthog

1.

spoon p___ ___le tea

_____

2.

coat shoes rain snow

_____

3.

air box mail

_____

4.

neck shoe lace tie

_____

Find the word that you c___ ___t together with *meal* to make a compound word.
Mark the space to show yo___ ___nswer.

5. _____ meal

⊂⊃ dinner
⊂⊃ oat
⊂⊃ book

6. meal _____

⊂⊃ time
⊂⊃ spoon
⊂⊃ napkin

Notes for Home: Your child reviewed compo___ ___d words—words that are made up of two smaller words, such as *warthog*. **Home Activity** ___ith your child, use the words listed above to make up other compound words such as *teaspo___ ___r snowshoes.*

face   twice   cage   huge   page   tease

Change one or two letters in each word to make a word from the box.
Write the new word on the line.

1. please _____

2. hugs _____

3. pale _____

4. slice _____

Write the word from the box to match each picture.

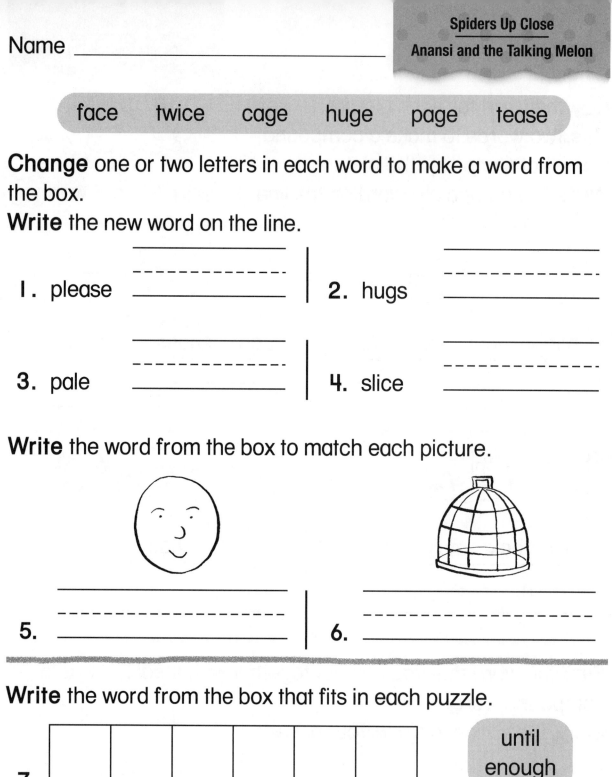

5. _____

6. _____

Write the word from the box that fits in each puzzle.

7. ⬜⬜⬜⬜⬜⬜

8. ⬜⬜⬜⬜

until
enough

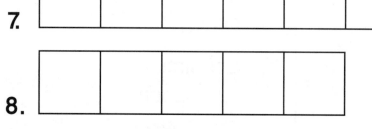

Notes for Home: Your child spelled words that end with *ce, ge,* and *se,* such as *face, cage,* and *tease,* and two frequently used words: *until, enough.* **Home Activity:** Have your child make new words that end with *ce, ge,* or *se* by changing one or two letters in each word.

Family Times

How I Beat the Giants

Play Ball

Work Together Now!

I see fans yelling in the crowd.
I hear shouting. They're getting loud.
We are clapping. We are proud.
Watch how we work together!

I see a pitcher on the mound.
I see a player running around.
I see a baseball hitting the ground.
Watch how we work together!

I see a catcher crouching down.
I see an umpire with a frown.
I see our player dressed in brown.
Watch how we work together!

This rhyme includes words your child is working with in school: words with *ou* and *ow* (*loud, crowd*) and words with double consonants followed by *-ed* and *-ing* endings (*running*). After singing "Work Together Now!," make a list showing words with *ou* and *ow*.

(fold here)

Name: _____

You are your child's first and best teacher!

Here are ways to help your child practice skills while having fun!

Day 1 Name a word with *ou* or *ow* that has the same vowel sound as *house* and *crown*. Challenge your child to name a word that rhymes with it and has the same spelling for the vowel sound, such as *house/mouse* and *crown/frown*.

Day 2 Use hand puppets or stuffed animals to make up a scene where two characters talk. Try to include these words: *been, friends, show, since,* and *those.*

Day 3 Read or tell a story to your child. Have your child summarize what happens in the story using two or three sentences.

Day 4 With your child, come up with a list of action words, such as *run, hop, leap,* and *sing.* Then take turns acting out each word.

Day 5 Help your child write a paragraph that tells a brief story. The story should describe real or make-believe people working together.

Read with your child EVERY DAY!

Verb Match-Up

Materials index cards, markers

Game Directions

1. Use index cards to write the pairs of related verbs shown on page 3.

2. Mix the cards and spread each one face down on a table or the floor.

3. Players take turns turning over two cards at a time, trying to match up verb pairs.

4. Players keep matching pairs of verb cards. If a match is not made, the players return cards to their original positions.

5. Play until all matches are made. The player with the most pairs wins!

bat	batted	get	getting
grip	gripped	nod	nodded
pet	petting	rub	rubbed
run	running	sit	sitting
stop	stopped	win	winning

Read each sentence.
Circle the word with the same vowel sound as **cow** or **house**.
Write the word on the line.

cow   house

1. I play baseball near my house.

2. We are the best team in town.

3. We are the Brown Bears.

4. I play in the outfield.

5. I went down to the park.

6. There wasn't a cloud in the sky.

7. The crowd was cheering.

8. My teammates shouted too.

9. We were about to win!

10. I hit the ball out of the park!

Notes for Home: Your child read and wrote words with the same vowel sound as *cow* and *house* spelled *ow* and *ou*. **Home Activity:** Ask your child to draw pictures representing as many *ou* and *ow* words as possible. Work together to label each picture.

Phonics: Vowel Diphthongs *ou, ow* **167**

Name _____

Read each word.
Find the base word.
Write the base word on the line.

stop + -ed = stopp**ed**   hop + -ing = hopp**ing**

1. sitting _____

2. gripped _____

3. running _____

4. nodded _____

5. shopped _____

6. spinning _____

7. getting _____

8. hitting _____

Add -ed and **-ing** to each base word.
Write the new words on the line.

+ -ed	+ -ing
9. bat _____	_____
10. clip _____	_____

Notes for Home: Your child read and wrote words whose final consonants are doubled before adding the endings -ed and -ing. **Home Activity:** Read a story together. Ask your child to point out words with -ed and -ing that have had their final consonants doubled.

Pick a word from the box to finish each sentence.
Write the word on the line.

been   friends   show   since   those

1. Tom and I are best _____ .

2. We have _____ pals for a long time.

3. We don't know _____ new boys.

4. They have only lived here _____ last night.

5. We will _____ them how to play!

Notes for Home: This week your child is learning to read the words *been, friends, show, since,* and *those.* **Home Activity:** Encourage your child to write sentences about his or her best friend using these words.

Name _____

Read the story.
Answer the questions.

A New Bike for Matt

Matt had a bike. He rode his bike all over.

One day, Matt left his bike out. The next day, the bike was gone!

Matt wanted a new bike.

He did extra chores around the house. He cut the grass. Soon Matt had enough money.

Matt's dad was proud. Matt got his new bike. Now Matt always puts it in a safe place!

1. What did Matt want?

_____
- -
_____

2. Why did he want it?

_____
- -
_____

3. What did he do to get it?

_____
- -
_____
_____
- -
_____

Notes for Home: Your child summarized what happened in a story. *Home Activity:* Watch a video or TV show with your child. Encourage your child to summarize what happened in the story in a few sentences.

170 Summarizing

Level 2.1

Name _____

fen**ce**   sta**ge**   hou**se**   no**se**

Circle the word for each picture.

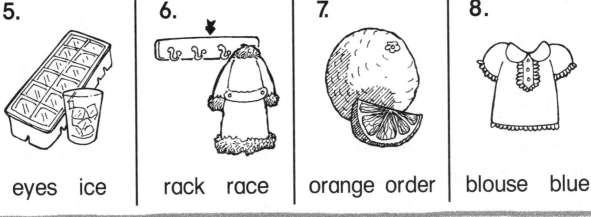

1.

mouse   moth

2.

face   fact

3.

rose   rope

4.

cake   cage

5.

eyes   ice

6.

rack   race

7.

orange   order

8.

blouse   blue

Find the word that has the same ending sound as the picture.
Mark the space to show your answer.

9. ⬭ host
　　 ⬭ hose
　　 ⬭ hotel

10. ⬭ test
　　 ⬭ taste
　　 ⬭ tease

 Notes for Home: Your child reviewed words that end in *ce, ge,* and *se.* **Home Activity:** Write *fence, stage, house,* and *nose* in a row across the top of a sheet of paper. Encourage your child to think of at least two more words that have the same ending sound as each word.

| hugged | hugging | nodded | nodding | skipped | skipping |

Add -ed or **-ing** to each word below to make a word from the box.
Write the new word on the line.

	Add -ed	**Add -ing**
hug	1. _____	2. _____
nod	3. _____	4. _____
skip	5. _____	6. _____

Pick a word from the box to finish each sentence.
Write the word on the line.

7. We are _____ rope.

8. Before I left, I _____ my friends.

Pick a word from the box to match each clue.
Write the word on the line.

| since those |

9. not these

_____

10. from then until now

_____

Notes for Home: Your child practiced spelling words that end with *-ed* and *-ing* and two frequently used words: *since, those*. **Home Activity:** Have your child use each spelling word in a sentence. Work together to write each sentence.

Name _____

Part I: Vocabulary

Find the word that best fits in each sentence.
Mark the space for your answer.

1. Scott hit the _____ hard.
   - ⬭ hundred
   - ⬭ baseball
   - ⬭ terrible

2. Ken was _____ the ball fast.
   - ⬭ going
   - ⬭ pitching
   - ⬭ peeling

3. Lina _____ from her trip yesterday.
   - ⬭ returned
   - ⬭ exclaimed
   - ⬭ followed

4. I will make a cake for you _____ it is your birthday.
   - ⬭ after
   - ⬭ until
   - ⬭ since

5. I like _____ apples better than these red ones.
   - ⬭ terrible
   - ⬭ those
   - ⬭ enough

© Scott Foresman 2

Part 2: Comprehension

Read each question.
Mark the space for your answer.

6. When it was Lionel's turn at bat, he —
   - ⬭ swung and missed.
   - ⬭ threw the ball to Ellen.
   - ⬭ hit the ball over the fence.

7. When he heard the crash, Lionel felt —
   - ⬭ terrible.
   - ⬭ glad.
   - ⬭ surprised.

8. Lionel and his friends will —
   - ⬭ pay for the broken window.
   - ⬭ help Mr. Barrie fix the window.
   - ⬭ never play baseball again.

9. Which sentence best tells what happens in this story?
   - ⬭ When Lionel breaks a window, all his friends help him.
   - ⬭ Max said that he hit the ball over the fence.
   - ⬭ Lionel tries to play baseball, but his friends know he is not very good.

10. If Lionel lost his coat, his friends probably would —
    - ⬭ tell his parents.
    - ⬭ laugh at him.
    - ⬭ help him find it.

STOP

**Add 's or ' to the word in ( ) to show
who owns something.
Write the new words on the lines below.**

Joe**'s** bat

---

1. This is my _____ cap. (sister)

2. Here are the _____ bats. (girls)

3. Here are the _____ couches. (teams)

4. Where is _____ mitt? (Jan)

5. I found the _____ missing ball. (boys)

6. How was _____ game? (Kim)

Find the word that shows who owns something.
Mark the space to show your answer.

7.	8.	9.	10.
⬭ crowds	⬭ fan	⬭ girls	⬭ kitten's
⬭ crowd	⬭ fans'	⬭ girl	⬭ kittens
⬭ crowd's	⬭ fans	⬭ girls'	⬭ kitten

Notes for Home: Your child reviewed possessives—words that show ownership or belonging.
Home Activity: Read a story together. Ask your child to point out any possessive words. Make
sure your child can tell the difference between possessive words and contractions.

Name _____

| hugged hugging nodded nodding skipped skipping |

Chook tho cpolling of oaoh word bolow.
If the word is correct, **write** it on the line.
If the word is wrong, **correct** it and **write** it on the line.

1. skiped

_____
_____

2. huged

_____
_____

3. hugging

_____
_____

4. noding

_____
_____

5. nodded

_____
_____

6. skiping

_____
_____

Pick a word from the box to finish each sentence.
Write the word on the line.

since
those

_____

7. I have been playing baseball _____ I was five.

_____

8. I play with _____ boys over there.

Notes for Home: Your child spelled words that end with *-ed* and *-ing* and two frequently-used words: *since, those.* **Home Activity:** Work with your child to write a story using these spelling words about a group of friends.

Family Times

People, People, Everywhere!

The Storykeeper

Our Guard Clark

There is a guard named Clark.
He drives around the park.
Clark patrols the neighborhood.
He works when it gets dark.

A party in the park,
Will start when it gets dark.
We've baked a lot of tasty tarts.
We're saving one for Clark.

We're making Clark a card,
Because he worked so hard.
When Clark is done, he'll park his car.
He is a super guard.

This rhyme includes words your child is working with in school: words with *ar* (*park*) and verbs that end in *-ed* and *-ing*. Sing "Our Guard Clark" with your child. Together, make a list of the words with *ar*. Then think of other *ar* words that rhyme with the words listed.

(fold here)

Name: _____

You are your child's first and best teacher!

Here are ways to help your child practice skills while having fun!

Day 1 Make a list of verbs (words that show action) that end in *e*, such as *race*, *ride*, or *move*. Read each one aloud. Ask your child to spell the word with an *-ed* or *-ing* ending.

Day 2 Work with your child to draw a picture and write a caption using the words *children*, *city*, *high*, *place*, and *room*.

Day 3 When reading together, show your child how to figure out the meaning of unfamiliar words by using context clues in nearby words, phrases, or pictures.

Day 4 Ask your child how he or she feels today. Help your child write a poem that expresses these feelings.

Day 5 Go for a walk with your child. Have your child make up sentences that describe the actions that he or she sees. Listen for the correct use of verbs to describe the actions by one person and the actions by more than one person.

Read with your child EVERY DAY!

ar Cover Up

Materials 6 buttons per player, paper, pencil, bag

Game Directions

1. Copy the words with *ar* below on slips of paper. Put the words in a bag.

2. Take turns choosing a word and reading it aloud.

3. If the word appears on a player's game card, the player puts a button on it.

4. The first player to get 4 buttons in a row (across, down, or diagonally) wins!

Words with *ar*
arm, art, bark, barn, car, card, cart, Clark, dark, dart, farm, hard, harm, jar, mark, park, part, star, stars, start, tar, tart, yard, yarn

car	hard	jar	tart
yard	mark	art	farm
star	arm	card	barn
cart	tar	Clark	bark

mark	car	part	yard
harm	start	hard	dark
barn	yarn	stars	cart
dart	card	park	arm

Name _____

Circle the word for each picture.

b<u>ar</u>k

1. pair
   park

2. barn
   band

3. arm
   hair

4. yarn
   yam

5. hard
   herd

6. cold
   card

7. stare
   star

8. cat
   cart

9. car
   care

10. jar
    jam

 Notes for Home: Your child read words that contain the letters *ar* that represent the vowel sound in *car*. **Home Activity:** Name several words that contain *ar*. Challenge your child to think of a word that rhymes with each one.

Name _____

Add the ending to each word.
Write the new word on the line.

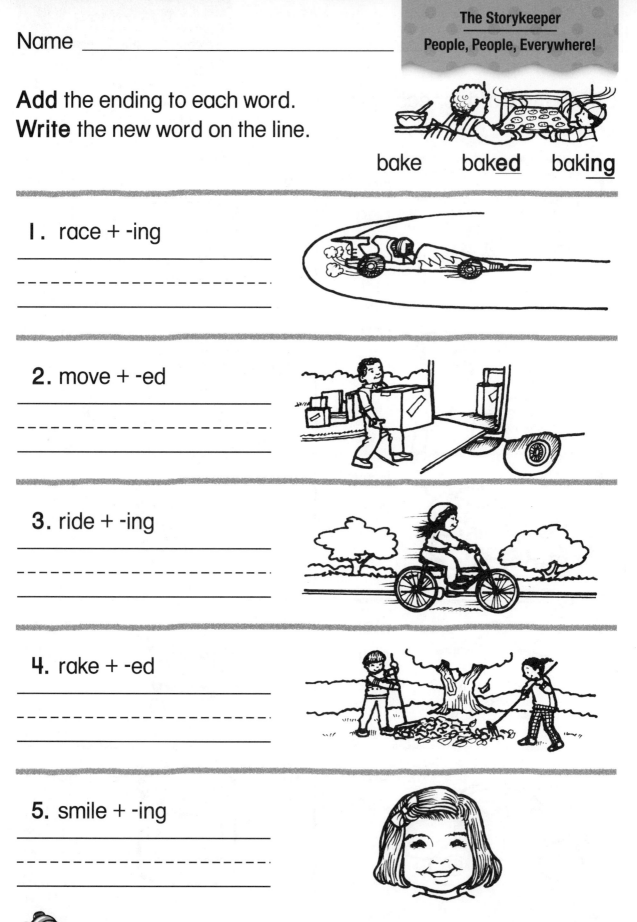

bake   bak**ed**   bak**ing**

1. race + -ing

_____
- - - - - - - - - - - - - - - - - - - -
_____

2. move + -ed

_____
- - - - - - - - - - - - - - - - - - - -
_____

3. ride + -ing

_____
- - - - - - - - - - - - - - - - - - - -
_____

4. rake + -ed

_____
- - - - - - - - - - - - - - - - - - - -
_____

5. smile + -ing

_____
- - - - - - - - - - - - - - - - - - - -
_____

Notes for Home: Your child wrote action words that drop the final *e* when adding the endings *-ed* and *-ing*. **Home Activity:** Encourage your child to make up a silly song using three or more of the action words on this page. Together write the words to the song and perform it.

Pick a word from the box to finish each sentence.
Write the word on the line.

children	city	high	place	room

1. I live in the _____ .

2. My home is way up _____ .

3. I have my own _____ .

4. I play with lots of _____ here.

5. It's a great _____ to live!

Notes for Home: This week your child is learning to read the words *children, city, high, place,* and *room.* ***Home Activity:*** Challenge your child to make up a story using all five of these words. Then, make a picture book of the story together.

Look at the picture.
Read the sentence with the underlined word.
Pick the word from the box to finish the second sentence.
Write the word on the line.

| boat | car | cried | run | sells |

The <u>vendor</u> has flowers for sale.
_____
- - - - - - - - - - - -
1. A *vendor* _____ things.

We took a <u>ferry</u> across the water.
_____
- - - - - - - - - - - -
2. A *ferry* is a _____ .

The unhappy baby <u>wailed</u>.
_____
- - - - - - - - - - - -
3. *Wailed* means the same as _____ .

My mom <u>dashed</u> outside quickly.
_____
- - - - - - - - - - - -
4. To *dash* means to _____ .

We rode in a <u>taxi</u>.
_____
- - - - - - - - - - - -
5. A *taxi* is a kind of _____ .

Notes for Home: Your child used context clues (words that surround an unfamiliar word and help explain its meaning) to figure out the meanings of words. *Home Activity:* Ask your child to point out unfamiliar words in a story. Together, use context clues to help figure out their meanings.

fl**ow**ers

ho<u>u</u>se

Circle the word for each picture.

1.	2.	3.	4.
town twin	most mouse	round rope	crown ʔre

5.	6.	7.	8.
clown crow	front frown	couch coach	grow gown

Find the word that has the same vowel sound as 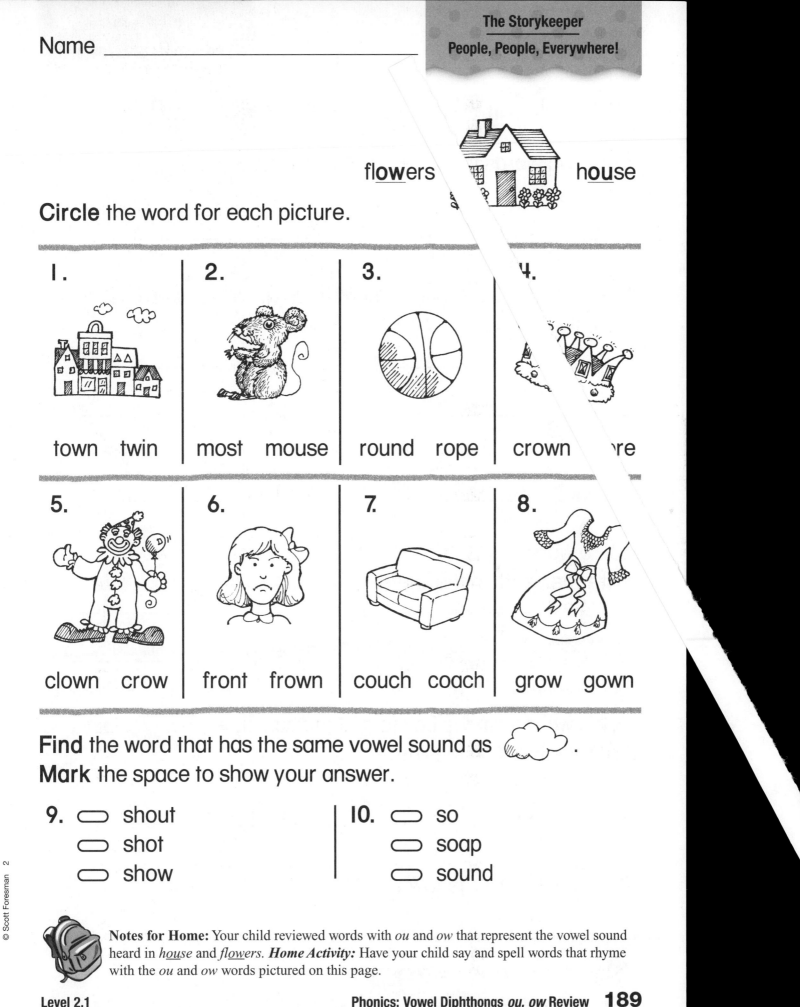 .
Mark the space to show your answer.

9. ⬭ shout
   ⬭ shot
   ⬭ show

10. ⬭ so
    ⬭ soap
    ⬭ sound

Notes for Home: Your child reviewed words with *ou* and *ow* that represent the vowel sound heard in *house* and *flowers*. **Home Activity:** Have your child say and spell words that rhyme with the *ou* and *ow* words pictured on this page.

arm   barn   farm   hard   park   start

Write two words from the box that rhyme with **harm**.

_____   _____

1. _____   2. _____

Pick a word from the box that rhymes with each word below.
Write the word on the line.

_____   _____

3. yarn _____   4. part _____

_____   _____

5. card _____   6. dark _____

Pick a word that is the opposite of each word below.
Write the word on the line.

_____   _____

7. soft _____   8. stop _____

Pick a word from the box to match each clue.   city   place
Write the word on the line.

_____

9. It rhymes with *face*.   _____

_____

10. It is a very large town. _____

Notes for Home: Your child spelled words with the *r*-controlled vowel *ar* where the letter *r* changes the vowel sound, as well as two frequently used words: *city, place.* **Home Activity:** Work with your child to write simple rhymes using these spelling words.

Name _____

Part 1: Vocabulary

Find the word that best fits in each sentence.
Mark the space for your answer.

1. My kite will fly very _____ .
    ▢ ripe   ▢ place   ▢ high

2. The _____ played in the park.
    ▢ wheel   ▢ children   ▢ country

3. There is not enough _____ for all of us.
    ▢ room   ▢ bottle   ▢ patch

4. Rose was _____ the leaks in the house.
    ▢ dashing   ▢ sealing   ▢ pitching

5. Dick lives in the _____ .
    ▢ city   ▢ surface   ▢ thumb

Part 2: Comprehension

Read each question.
Mark the space for your answer.

6. In this story, people wait in line to —
   - ⬭ get on the bus.
   - ⬭ buy tickets.
   - ⬭ eat food.

7. You can tell from the clues in the story that vendors —
   - ⬭ sell things.
   - ⬭ clean the streets.
   - ⬭ ride in cars.

8. You can tell that the people in this story are very —
   - ⬭ busy.
   - ⬭ tired.
   - ⬭ happy.

9. How is the country different from the city?
   - ⬭ There are more cars and noise.
   - ⬭ There are more people.
   - ⬭ There is more room, and it is quiet.

10. What happens when many people move to the country?
    - ⬭ They do not work.
    - ⬭ They ride in taxis.
    - ⬭ The country starts to look like a city.

Name _____

Add -ed and **-ing** to each word below.
Write the new words on the lines.

drop dropp**ing** dropp**ed**

	Add -ed		Add -ing
rub	1. _____		2. _____
fix	3. _____		4. _____
jog	5. _____		6. _____
hop	7. _____		8. _____

Find the word where yo_ _ould double the last consonant
before adding **-ed** or **-**_
Mark the space to s_ _our answer.

9. ⬭ help
   ⬭ drum
   ⬭ ask

10. ⬭ stop
    ⬭ work
    ⬭ mix

Home: Your child reviewed words that end in *-ed* and *-ing*. **Home Activity:** Read a
__ether. Look for words that end in *-ed* or *-ing*. Challenge your child to tell you what
_se word is, for example, *stop* is the base word for *stopped* and *stopping*.

arm   barn   farm   hard   park   start

Pick a word from the box to match each picture.
Write the word on the line.

1. _____
   - - - - - - - - - -
   _____

2. _____
   - - - - - - - - - -
   _____

3. _____
   - - - - - - - - - -
   _____

Change one letter in each word to make a word from the box.
Write the new word on the line.

4. stars
   _____
   - - - - - - - - - -
   _____

5. card
   _____
   - - - - - - - - - -
   _____

6. yarn
   _____
   - - - - - - - - - -
   _____

Pick a word from the box to finish each tongue twister.
Write the word on the line.

city   place

7. Polly picked a pretty _____ to play.

8. Six seals sit sipping tea in the _____ .

Notes for Home: Your child spelled words with the *r*-controlled vowel *ar* where the letter *r* changes the vowel sound, as well as two frequently-used words: *city, place.* **Home Activity:** Work with your child to write a poem which includes these spelling words.

Family Times

New Best Friends

Wanted: Best Friend

My Friend Scooter

I've got a friend named Scooter.
I'm meeting him at noon.
He's bringing his new poodle.
We will go swimming soon.

We're bringing gooey noodles.
We're bringing lots of food.
We're bringing chewy cashews,
In case we're in the mood.

Let's not forget our soup spoons.
To use this afternoon.
We'll have a little party.
Let's bring along balloons.

This rhyme includes words your child is working with in school: words with *ew*, *oo*, and *ou* (*new*, *spoons*, *soup*) and contractions. (*Let's*, *We'll*) Read aloud "My Friend Scooter" with your child. Make a list of the contractions in the rhyme and identify the two words each contraction represents.

(fold here)

Name: _____

You are your child's first and best teacher!

Here are ways to help your child practice skills while having fun!

Day 1 Write the letters *n't*, *'s*, *'ll*, *'m*, *'d*, *'re*, and *'ve* on slips of paper. Place them in a hat or bowl. Have your child pick a slip and name a contraction that uses those letters.

Day 2 Work with your child to create a word search puzzle using these words that your child is learning to read: *across*, *best*, *either*, *sometimes*, and *toward*.

Day 3 Read a story with your child. Review key events in the story and ask your child what caused each event to happen.

Day 4 Ask your child to choose a favorite character from a book or movie. Help your child write a paragraph describing how this character looks and behaves.

Day 5 Your child is practicing reading aloud. Encourage him or her to choose a favorite story or poem and read it aloud, using the punctuation to help pace his or her reading.

Read with your child EVERY DAY!

Spinning Vowels

Materials paper circle, paper clip,
pencil, 1 button per player

Game Directions

1. Make a simple spinner as shown.

2. Take turns spinning a letter pair and writing a word
that uses *ew*, *oo*, or *ou* and has the vowel sound
in *new*, *soon*, or *soup*.

3. If the word is written correctly, the player moves
his or her button the number of spaces shown on
the spinner.

4. The first player to reach the end wins!

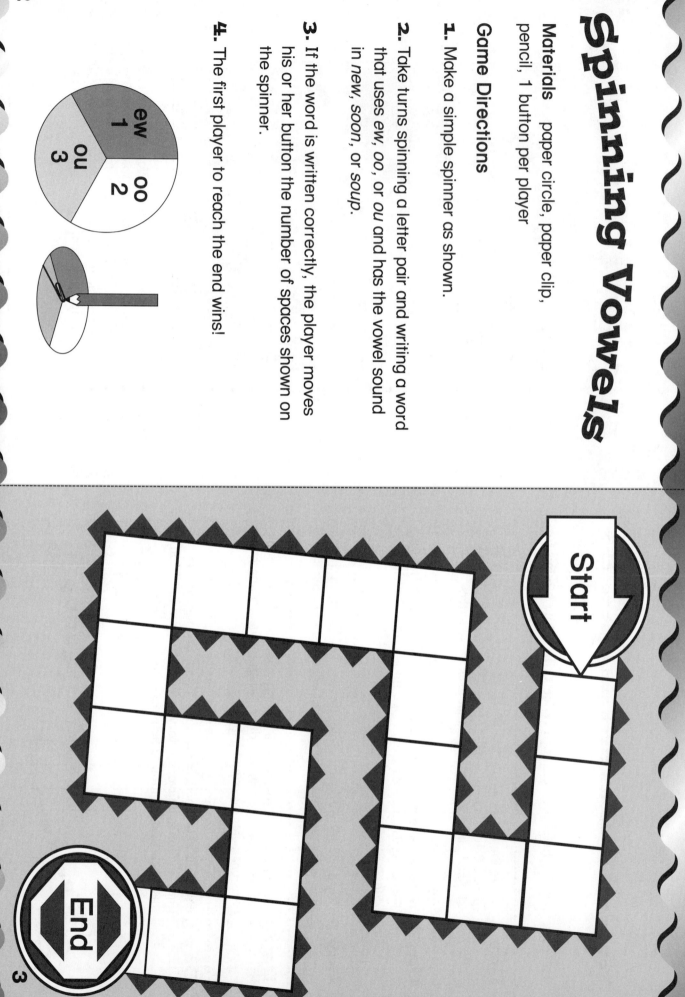

Start

End

Name _____

Circle all the words that have the same vowel sound as **new**.

 Y<u>ou</u> have **n<u>ew</u> b<u>oo</u>ts**!

1. Barb and I have soup every day at noon.

2. You can sit with us too.

3. We'd like a few more friends in the group.

4. I knew making new friends was fun!

Draw a picture of a zoo.
Write a sentence for your picture.

5.

_____

- -

_____

- -

_____

 Notes for Home: Your child identified words spelled with *ew, oo,* and *ou* that have the same vowel sound. **Home Activity:** Encourage your child to make up a poem or song using as many rhyming words containing this vowel sound as possible.

Name _____

Pick the contraction that is formed
from each pair of words.
Write the contraction on the line.

It is happy.
It's happy.

don't	he'd	I'll	I'm	let's
she's	that's	we're	you're	you've

1. you + are

_____

- - - - - - - - - -

_____

2. that + is

_____

- - - - - - - - - -

_____

3. I + will

_____

- - - - - - - - - -

_____

4. he + had

_____

- - - - - - - - - -

_____

5. do + not

_____

- - - - - - - - - -

_____

6. you + have

_____

- - - - - - - - - -

_____

7. let + us

_____

- - - - - - - - - -

_____

8. I + am

_____

- - - - - - - - - -

_____

9. she + has

_____

- - - - - - - - - -

_____

10. we + are

_____

- - - - - - - - - -

_____

Notes for Home: Your child practiced forming contractions. *Home Activity:* Work with your child
to make a simple set of flashcards with a word pair (such as *do not*) on one side and the matching
contraction (such as *don't*) on the other. Help your child practice contractions using the flash cards.

Part 1: Vocabulary

Find the word that best fits in each sentence.
Mark the space for your answer.

1. I get to stay up late _____ .
   ⬭ sometimes   ⬭ around   ⬭ either

2. Josie _____ that she felt sick.
   ⬭ dumped   ⬭ complained   ⬭ returned

3. Mel rode her bike _____ me.
   ⬭ through   ⬭ across   ⬭ toward

4. Dad walked _____ the street.
   ⬭ since   ⬭ across   ⬭ sometimes

5. You can _____ come with us or stay home.
   ⬭ best   ⬭ once   ⬭ either

Part 2: Comprehension

Read each question.
Mark the space for your answer.

6. Why did Mouse go home?
   - ⬭ Cat did not want to play crazy eights.
   - ⬭ Cat had a new friend.
   - ⬭ Mouse was tired of games.

7. Cat called *The Hollow Log Gazette* because he wanted to —
   - ⬭ buy a newspaper.
   - ⬭ try to find a friend.
   - ⬭ buy a new game.

8. Who made the biggest mess in Cat's house?
   - ⬭ Raccoon
   - ⬭ Mouse
   - ⬭ Mole

9. When Cat and Mouse play crazy eights, Cat will —
   - ⬭ try to find a new friend.
   - ⬭ ask Otter to come and watch.
   - ⬭ be nicer to Mouse.

10. What did Cat learn in this story?
    - ⬭ Mouse would never come back again.
    - ⬭ Mouse was his best friend after all.
    - ⬭ He could not beat Mouse at checkers.

Name _____

Add -ed and **-ing** to each word below.
Write the new words on the lines.

smil~~e~~ + -ed = smil**ed**
smil~~e~~ + -ing = smil**ing**

Add -ed	Add -ing
race	1. _____	2. _____
hop	3. _____	4. _____
move	5. _____	6. _____
use	7. _____	8. _____

Find the new word that is formed by adding **-ed** or **-ing**.
Mark the space to show your answer.

9. dance + -ed =
 ⬭ danceed
 ⬭ danced
 ⬭ dancced

10. give + -ing =
 ⬭ giving
 ⬭ givving
 ⬭ giveing

Notes for Home: Your child reviewed words that end with *-ed* and *-ing*. **Home Activity:** Ask your child to draw pictures showing the actions named by two or more of the words above. Help your child write a sentence to go with each picture.

| I'll | I'm | can't | didn't | he's | she's |

Pick a word from the box to replace the underlined words.
Write the word on the line.

1. <u>I am</u> glad I met Gina and Tony. _____

2. I <u>did not</u> know them last year. _____

3. <u>He is</u> so funny. _____

4. <u>She is</u> funny too. _____

5. We <u>cannot</u> stop laughing sometimes. _____

6. <u>I will</u> see them both tomorrow. _____

Pick a word from the box to finish each sentence.
Write the word on the line.

| best | sometimes |

7. Carlos is my _____ friend.

8. We _____ play baseball together.

Notes for Home: Your child spelled contractions such as *she's* and *didn't* and two frequently used words: *best, sometimes.* **Home Activity:** Name the two words that each contraction represents. Have your child name the contraction and write it.

Family Times

Four Clues for Chee   **Young Cam Jansen and the Dinosaur Game**

Doris and Boris

On a street corner,
At Court Street and Fourth,
Doris is running.
She hurries north.

She's a reporter,
Exploring for clues.
She takes her own notes,
Recording the news.

She looks for more clues,
And spies a good source.
The source for her story,
Is Boris, of course!

Boris gives Doris
A clue she can use.
She writes her story,
Reporting the news.

This rhyme includes words your child is working with in school: words with *or* or *ore*, and *our* (*for*, *more*, *source*) and verbs that change *y* to *i* before adding an ending (*hurries*). Sing "Doris and Boris" with your child. Underline all the words with the vowel sound heard in *Doris* spelled *or*, *ore*, and *our*.

(fold here)

Name: _____

You are your child's first and best teacher!

Here are ways to help your child practice skills while having fun!

Day 1   Make a list of words that have the same vowel sound heard in *storm* spelled *or*, *ore*, *oor*, and *our*, such as *corner*, *more*, *door*, and *your*.

Day 2   Make up a fun song using the words children are learning to read this week: *bring, brought, next, picture,* and *read*.

Day 3   Watch a TV show with your child. Then, ask your child to tell what they learned about the characters in the show.

Day 4   Your child is learning about the importance of a story's title. Read a short story to your child without telling him or her the title. Brainstorm possible titles with your child.

Day 5   Practice using nonverbal communication with your child by playing charades. Take turns acting out a word or phrase for others to guess.

Read with your child EVERY DAY!

Add -ed or -es

Materials index cards, markers, coin, 1 button per player

Game Directions

1. Write the verbs shown below on index cards.

2. Take turns picking a card and flipping the coin. If heads, add -ed to the verb. If tails, add -es. Spell the new word aloud.

3. If a player spells the word correctly, the player tosses a button on the gameboard to try to earn points.

4. The first player to earn 15 points wins!

Verbs

carry, try, hurry, cry, marry, fry, worry, copy, dry

Earn 2 points!				Earn 1 point!
	Earn 3 points!		Take 2 points from other players!	Lose 2 points!
Take 2 points from other players!			Earn 2 points!	
	Earn 1 point!	Lose 4 points!	Earn 6 points!	Lose 2 points!

Name _____

Pick a word from the box to match each clue.
Write the word on the line.

tore	store	horn	door
pour	fork	corn	sport

Order in the c**our**t!

1. something you knock on

   _____

2. something on a bull

   _____

3. ripped

   _____

4. a place where you buy things

   _____

5. something to eat with

   _____

6. you can play or watch this

   _____

7. something you do with a pitcher

   _____

8. something you can pop and eat

   _____

Notes for Home: Your child read and wrote words with *or, ore, oor,* and *our* where the letter *r* changes the vowel sound. ***Home Activity:*** Ask your child to think of other words that rhyme with each of the words in the box.

© Scott Foresman 2

Name _____

Add -ed and **-es** to each word below.
Write the new words on the lines.

The babies cr**ied**.
She cr**ies** loudly.

Word	+ -ed	+ -es
carry	1. _____	2. _____
hurry	3. _____	4. _____
dry	5. _____	6. _____
try	7. _____	8. _____
study	9. _____	10. _____

Notes for Home: Your child wrote words in which the final *y* changes to *i* before adding *-ed or -es*.
Home Activity: Challenge your child to use several of the words in the second and third columns in
sentences. Check whether your child uses *-ed* for past actions and *-es* for present actions.

Name _____

Pick a word from the box to finish each sentence.
Write the word on the line.

bring	brought	next	picture	read

_____
- - - - - - - - - - - - - - - - - - -

1. What kind of present did you _____ Lil?

_____
- - - - - - - - - - - - - - - -

2. I _____ a book.

_____
- - - - - - - - - - - - - - - - - -

3. I hope she hasn't _____ it yet.

_____
- - - - - - - - - - - - - - - - - -

4. It has a nice _____ of a cat on the cover.

_____
- - - - - - - - - - - - - - - -

5. Lil will open my present _____ !

Notes for Home: This week your child is learning to read the words *bring, brought, next, picture,* and *read.* **Home Activity:** Challenge your child to make up a story about a party using these words.

© Scott Foresman 2

Name _____

Write a word from the box to name each person.

| doctor | painter | teacher | vet |

1. I help sick people. I take care of them. I help them feel well.

   I am a _doctor_ .

2. I help you learn. I read lots of books. I work in a school.

   I am a _teacher_ .

3. I take care of cats and dogs. I help them feel well.

   I am a _____ .

4. I draw and paint. I use lots of pretty colors.

   I am a _____ .

Draw a picture of one of the people described.
Show something this person does.

5.

Notes for Home: Your child identified characters based on things they say and do.
Home Activity: Read a story with your child. Name characters from the story. Have your child describe each character and tell how he or she knows what the character is like.

© Scott Foresman 2

Look at the table of contents from a book of fairy tales.
Write the answer to each question.

Favorite Fairy Tales
Contents
Cinderella 3
Sleeping Beauty 10
Three Little Pigs 15
Rumpelstiltskin 21
Rapunzel 26

1. How many stories are in this book? _____

2. What is the name of the first story?

   _____

3. On what page does "Sleeping Beauty" start? _____

4. Which story comes before "Rumpelstiltskin"?

   _____

5. What is the name of the last story?

   _____

Notes for Home: Your child read a table of contents and answered questions about it. *Home Activity:* Look through books in your home or at the library. Compare different tables of contents and talk about the information each one shows.

Name _____

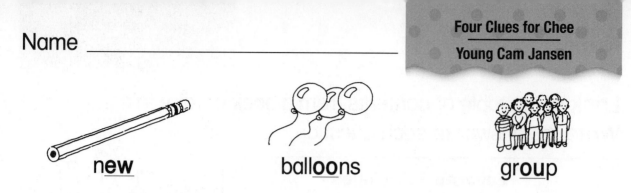

n**ew**   ball**oo**ns   gr**ou**p

Circle the word for each picture.

1.	2.	3.	4.
nose news	soup soap	moon mine	broom brim

5.	6.	7.	8.
school skill	stay stew	crew cry	spine spoon

Find the word that has the same vowel sound as the picture.
Mark the space to show your answer.

9. ⬭ few
   ⬭ feet
   ⬭ foot

10. ⬭ you
    ⬭ your
    ⬭ young

Notes for Home: Your child reviewed words with *ew, oo,* and *ou* that have the same vowel sound (*new, balloons,* and *group*). **Home Activity:** Say one of the words with *ew, oo,* or *ou* on this page, and ask your child to say a rhyming word spelled the same way.

Part 1: Vocabulary

Find the word that best fits in each sentence.
Mark the space for your answer.

1. Lee _____ a dog to school.
   - ⬭ drew
   - ⬭ giggled
   - ⬭ brought

2. Will you take a picture with my _____?
   - ⬭ order
   - ⬭ camera
   - ⬭ mirror

3. _____ were very big animals.
   - ⬭ Dinosaurs
   - ⬭ Scales
   - ⬭ Friends

4. Who is _____ in line?
   - ⬭ toward
   - ⬭ clean
   - ⬭ next

5. Les knew the _____ number.
   - ⬭ either
   - ⬭ exact
   - ⬭ between

GO ON ➤

Part 2: Comprehension

Read each question.
Mark the space for your answer.

6. What is special about Cam Jansen?
   - ⬭ She knows how to use a camera.
   - ⬭ She does not forget things.
   - ⬭ She gets lost.

7. What did the children do first?
   - ⬭ played musical chairs
   - ⬭ ate birthday cake
   - ⬭ wrote numbers on slips of paper

8. How did Cam know that Robert made his guess after the others?
   - ⬭ Robert told her he had guessed twice.
   - ⬭ There was some cake on the paper.
   - ⬭ Robert had the best guess.

9. How is Eric different from Robert?
   - ⬭ Eric wins every game.
   - ⬭ Eric shares the dinosaurs.
   - ⬭ Eric does not like cake.

10. Of all the children, Cam was best at —
    - ⬭ finding answers to questions.
    - ⬭ playing musical chairs.
    - ⬭ guessing the right numbers.

Put each pair of words together to make a contraction.
Write the contraction on the line.   I + am = **I'm**

1. do not

_____
- - - - - - - - - - - - -
_____

2. could not

_____
- - - - - - - - - - - - -
_____

3. that is

_____
- - - - - - - - - - - - -
_____

4. here is

_____
- - - - - - - - - - - - -
_____

5. I will

_____
- - - - - - - - - - - - -
_____

6. we are

_____
- - - - - - - - - - - - -
_____

7. let us

_____
- - - - - - - - - - - - -
_____

8. you are

_____
- - - - - - - - - - - - -
_____

Find the contraction that is made by putting each pair of words together.
Mark the space to show your answer.

9. we have
  ⬭ we've
  ⬭ wave
  ⬭ we'd

10. it is
  ⬭ its
  ⬭ its'
  ⬭ it's

Notes for Home: Your child reviewed contractions such as *don't, I'll,* and *couldn't.*
Home Activity: With your child, make a list of other contractions you know. For each
contraction you list, write the two words it represents.

Name _____

| door | corn | horse | more | pour | store |

Pick a word from the box to match each clue.
Write the word on the line.

1. an animal you can ride

_____

- - - - - - - - - - - - - -

_____

2. a greater amount

_____

- - - - - - - - - - - - - -

_____

3. a place to shop

_____

- - - - - - - - - - - - - -

_____

4. something you eat or pop

_____

- - - - - - - - - - - - - -

_____

5. something you knock on

_____

- - - - - - - - - - - - - -

_____

6. something you do to milk

_____

- - - - - - - - - - - - - -

_____

Pick a word from the box to finish each sentence.
Write the word on the line.

brought
picture

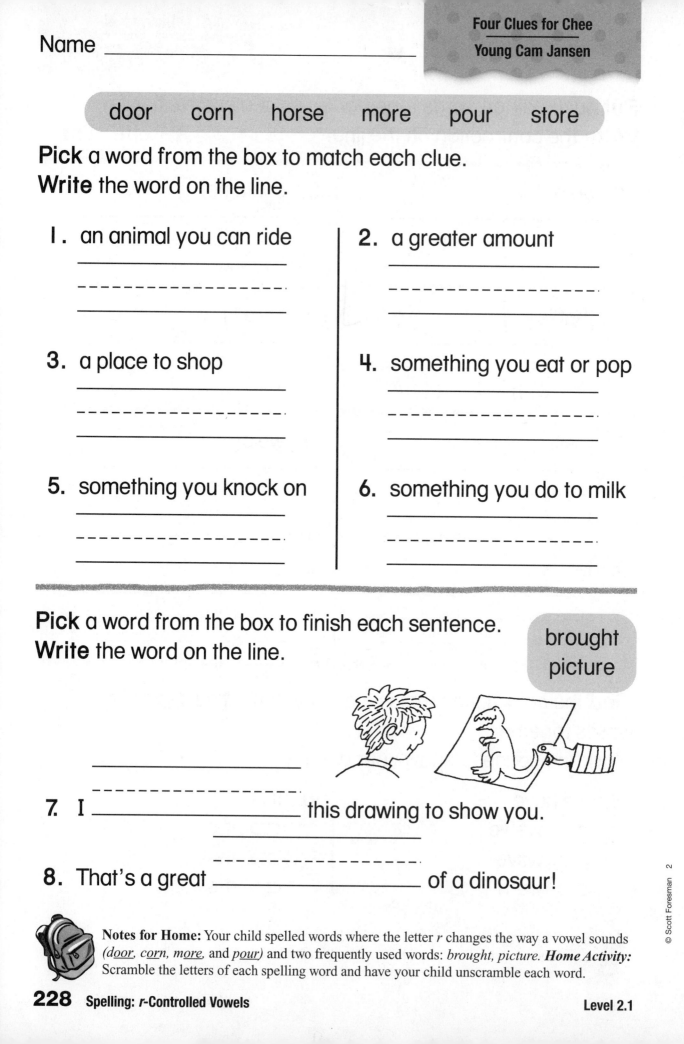

_____

- - - - - - - - - - - - - -

7. I _____ this drawing to show you.

_____

- - - - - - - - - - - - - -

8. That's a great _____ of a dinosaur!

Notes for Home: Your child spelled words where the letter *r* changes the way a vowel sounds (*door*, *corn*, *more*, and *pour*) and two frequently used words: *brought, picture.* **Home Activity:** Scramble the letters of each spelling word and have your child unscramble each word.

© Scott Foresman 2

Family Times

A Good Laugh For Cookie

Moonbear's Pet

When I Grow Older

My older sister likes to read a good book.
My older brother likes to stir and cook.

When I grow older, I could read this book.
When I grow older, I could learn to cook.

My older sister likes to fish in the brook.
My older brother likes to bait the hook.

When I grow older, I could fish in the brook.
When I grow older, I could bait the hook.

I am the youngest child of us all.
I look and listen because I'm small!

This rhyme includes words your child is working with in school: words with *oo* and *ou* (*book*, *could*) and words that end in *-er* and *-est*. Read aloud "When I Grow Older" with your child. Then, take turns comparing family members. For example: *My hair is longer than yours. But my sister has the longest hair of all.*

(fold here)

Name: _____

You are your child's first and best teacher!

Here are ways to help your child practice skills while having fun!

Day 1   Write the word *took* on the left side of a sheet of paper and the word *could* on the right side. List other words with *oo* and *ou* that have the same vowel sound as the word at the top of each column.

Day 2   Hold a reading bee with your child and his or her friends. Have the children read a word and use it in a sentence. Include these words: *beautiful, become, even, great,* and *together.*

Day 3   Watch a movie with your child. When you finish, encourage your child to tell what happened in the story using just a few sentences.

Day 4   Work with your child to write a paragraph comparing and contrasting two friends or family members.

Day 5   Make a set of flash cards with the verbs *is, are, was, were,* and *will be.* Have your child pick a card and use the verb in a sentence.

Read with your child EVERY DAY!

The Comparing Game

Materials paper circle, paper clip, pencil, marker

Game Directions

1. Make a simple spinner as shown.

2. Players take turns spinning and moving on the gameboard.

3. When a player lands on a space with a word, he or she must say and spell that word using -er and -est endings.

4. If the word is spelled correctly for both endings, the player follows the directions on the space. The first player to reach the end wins!

1	2
3	4

End			**tall** Spin again	
				wide Move forward 3 spaces
Start ↓				
big Move forward 2 spaces				
	little Move forward 4 spaces	**fat** Move forward 1 space		
small Spin again				

Pick a word from the box to finish each sentence.
Write the word on the line.

| beautiful | become | even | great | together |

_____
- - - - - - - - - - - - - - - -
1. They keep their pets _____ .

_____
- - - - - - - - - - - - - - - -
2. They have a _____ time with them.

_____
- - - - - - - - - - - - - - - -
3. They _____ feed them at the same time.

_____
- - - - - - - - - - - - - - - -
4. One day their pets will _____ frogs.

_____
- - - - - - - - - - - - - - - -
5. Frogs are not ugly. They're _____ .

Notes for Home: This week your child is learning to read the words *beautiful, become, even, great,* and *together.* **Home Activity:** Have your child use these sentences as models for writing his or her own sentences about a pet he or she has or would like to have.

Write a sentence that tells what each passage is mostly about.
Draw a picture that shows what each passage is mostly about.

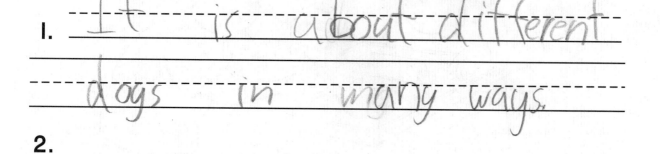

Dogs may be different in many ways.
Some dogs are long and thin. Some are small.
Some are very big.

✓

1. _It is about different_
   dogs in many ways.

2.

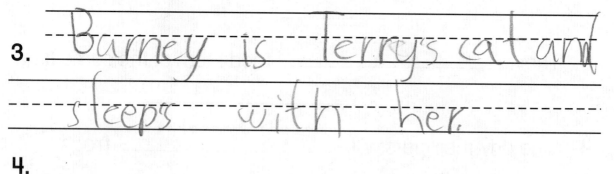

Barney is Terry's cat. Barney follows Terry everywhere.
He sleeps on her bed every night.
He even sits by her when she eats.

3. _Barney is Terry's cat and_
   sleeps with her.

4.

Notes for Home: Your child read a passage and wrote a sentence to tell what it was mostly about.
Home Activity: Talk about a story your child is familiar with. Ask him or her to tell what the
story is mostly about in just a few sentences.

The verbs **is, are, was, were,** and **will be** do not show action.
The verbs **is** and **are** tell about now.
The verbs **was** and **were** tell about the past.
The verb **will be** tells about the future.

Circle the correct verb to finish each sentence.
Write the verb on the line.

1. Tom _____ playing with his pup.

                                                                                                                  are
was

2. Tom and the pup _____ happy.

   were
was

3. Today, the pup _____ sleepy.

   is
was

4. Today, they _____ at home.

   is
are

5. Someday, the pup _____ big.

   were
will be

Notes for Home: Your child used the verbs *is, are, was, were,* and *will be* in sentences.
Home Activity: Write *Now, Past,* and *Future* on sheets of paper. Help your child write
sentences on each sheet, using the verbs *is, are, was, were,* and *will be.*

Pick a word from the box to match each clue.
Write the word on the line.

beautiful	become	bubbles
decide	paws	quite

1. ○ ○ ○

_____

_____

2. very pretty

_____

_____

3. to make up your mind

_____

_____

4. That dog made _____ a mess!

_____

_____

5. another name for a dog's feet

_____

_____

6. turn into

_____

_____

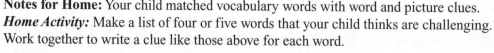

Notes for Home: Your child matched vocabulary words with word and picture clues.
Home Activity: Make a list of four or five words that your child thinks are challenging.
Work together to write a clue like those above for each word.

© Scott Foresman 2

th**orn**   c**ore**   d**oor**   f**our**

Circle the word for each picture.

1.	2.	3.	4.
acorn actor	corn coin	snore snare	floor flower

5.	6.	7.	8.
stare store	turn torn	hers horse	peer pour

Find the word that has the same vowel sound as the picture.
Mark the space to show your answer.

9. ⬭ stork
   ⬭ stock
   ⬭ stir

10. ⬭ firm
    ⬭ four
    ⬭ few

Notes for Home: Your child reviewed words that contain the *r*-controlled vowels *or, ore, oor,* and *our,* found in *th*o*rn, c*o*re, d*oo*r,* and *f*ou*r.* **Home Activity:** Ask your child to draw pictures illustrating some of the words on this page. Help your child label each picture.

© Scott Foresman   2

Name _____

| book | hood | shook | stood | took | wood |

Write three words from the box that rhyme with **good**.

1. _____ 2. _____ 3. _____

Write three words from the box that rhyme with **look**.

4. _____ 5. _____ 6. _____

Pick a word from the box to match each picture.
Write the word on the line.

7.

_____

8.

_____

Pick a word from the box to finish each sentence.
Write the word on the line.

become
even

9. When I read, I _____ part of the story.

10. I _____ pretend I am the hero!

Notes for Home: Your child spelled words with *oo* that have the same vowel sound heard in *book* and two frequently used words: *become, even.* **Home Activity:** Have your child use each spelling word in a sentence. Together, write each sentence.

Use words that help show how two things are alike or different.

Cats need water.
Dogs **also** need water.

Circle a word in ( ) to finish each sentence.

1. (Both/Two) cats and dogs like living with people.

2. Cats make good pets. But lions do (know/not).

3. Pets need love just (like/same) people do.

4. A dog's needs are (same/different) from a bird's needs.

Write a sentence that compares two animals.
Use the word **both** in your sentence.

5. _____

_____

_____

Notes for Home: Your child identified words that show comparisons and contrasts. *Home Activity:* Ask your child to compare and contrast two different animals. Have him or her tell how they are alike and how they are different.

© Scott Foresman 2

Name _Daniel Lane_

Circle a verb in ( ) to finish each sentence.

1. Today Jill and I (is /are) playing ball.

2. Jill (is / are) my best friend.

3. Tomorrow we (was / will be) at school.

4. Last week Jill (was / will be) sick.

5. But today she (is / are) feeling better.

6. Last year, Jill and I (are / were) not friends.

7. I (was / will be) living in a different town then.

8. I hope we (were / will be) friends forever!

Write two sentences about your friends.
Use one of these verbs in each sentence: *is, are, was, were,* and *will be.*

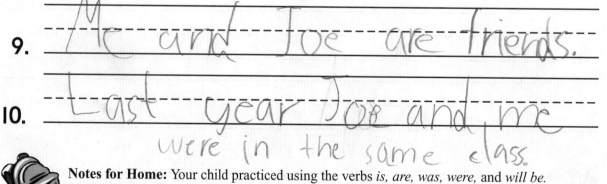

9. Me and Joe are friends.

10. Last year Joe and me were in the same class.

Notes for Home: Your child practiced using the verbs *is, are, was, were,* and *will be.*
Home Activity: Write these verbs on slips of paper. Take turns picking a verb and using it in a sentence.

Part 1: Vocabulary

Find the word that best fits in each sentence.
Mark the space for your answer.

1. Sue saw a _____ red bird.
   - mirror
   - beautiful
   - ripe

2. Ted will _____ a fireman when he grows up.
   - become
   - decide
   - keep

3. A dog has four _____ .
   - brains
   - tools
   - paws

4. Kat blew big _____ .
   - messages
   - bubbles
   - wheels

5. Ben is _____ tall for his age.
   - quite
   - around
   - between

GO ON

Part 2: Comprehension

Read each question.

Mark the space for your answer.

6. What happens first in this story?
   - ⬭ Moonbear goes shopping.
   - ⬭ Splash grows four legs.
   - ⬭ Moonbear finds a pet.

7. You can tell that Bear —
   - ⬭ likes his new pet a lot.
   - ⬭ does not take good care of his pet.
   - ⬭ is mean to his new pet.

8. Little Bird thought that Splash —
   - ⬭ should be in a pool.
   - ⬭ wanted to be a bird.
   - ⬭ was growing paws.

9. How did Splash get out of the pool?
   - ⬭ She hopped out.
   - ⬭ Someone took her out.
   - ⬭ She flew out.

10. This story is about two friends who learn that —
    - ⬭ they should not fight about silly things.
    - ⬭ everyone should be a bird.
    - ⬭ fish grow up to be frogs.

Add -ed to each verb.
Write the new word on the line.

cr̶y̶ + -es = cr**ies**

cr̶y̶ + -ed = cr**ied**

1. fry _____

2. help _____

3. try _____

4. reply _____

Add -es to each verb.
Write the new word on the line.

5. hurry _____

6. dry _____

7. fix _____

8. worry _____

Find the word where **-es** has been added to a verb.
Mark the space to show your answer.

9. ⬭ cars
   ⬭ carries
   ⬭ canes

10. ⬭ mares
    ⬭ marry
    ⬭ marries

Notes for Home: Your child reviewed words that end with -ed and -es, including words where the final y is changed to an i before -ed or -es is added. **Home Activity:** Ask your child to spell other words in which y changes to i before -ed or -es is added, such as bury, study, and carry.

Name _____

Find the words from the box in the puzzle.
They may go across or down.
Circle each word in the puzzle.
Write the words on the lines.

book	hood	shook
stood	took	wood

s	t	o	o	d	x	g	l	b	w
b	v	y	b	o	o	k	o	p	o
t	a	c	y	u	w	e	u	i	o
o	h	o	o	d	h	q	w	y	d
o	h	j	g	o	s	y	k	e	c
k	s	s	h	o	o	k	n	y	v

1. _____ 2. _____

3. _____ 4. _____

5. _____ 6. _____

Pick a word from the box to finish each sentence.
Write the word on the line.

become
even

7. A tadpole will _____ a frog.

8. It will _____ grow legs!

Notes for Home: Your child spelled words with the letters *oo* that have the same vowel sound heard in *book* and two frequently used words: *become, even.* **Home Activity:** Work with your child to write and illustrate a story using these spelling words.

244 Spelling: Vowel Pattern *oo*   **Level 2.1**

Name _____

Reading Log

Date	What is the title?	Who is the author?	What did you think of it?

Name _____

Reading Log

Date	What is the title?	Who is the author?	What did you think of it?

Name _____

Words I Can Now Read and Write

_____   _____
- - - - - - - - - - - - - - - - - - -   - - - - - - - - - - - - - - - - - - -
_____   _____

_____   _____
- - - - - - - - - - - - - - - - - - -   - - - - - - - - - - - - - - - - - - -
_____   _____

_____   _____
- - - - - - - - - - - - - - - - - - -   - - - - - - - - - - - - - - - - - - -
_____   _____

_____   _____
- - - - - - - - - - - - - - - - - - -   - - - - - - - - - - - - - - - - - - -
_____   _____

_____   _____
- - - - - - - - - - - - - - - - - - -   - - - - - - - - - - - - - - - - - - -
_____   _____

- - - - - - - - - - - - - - - - - - -
_____

_____
- - - - - - - - - - - - - - - - - - -
_____

Name _____

Correct each sentence.
Write it on the line.
Hint: Make sure that verbs are used correctly.

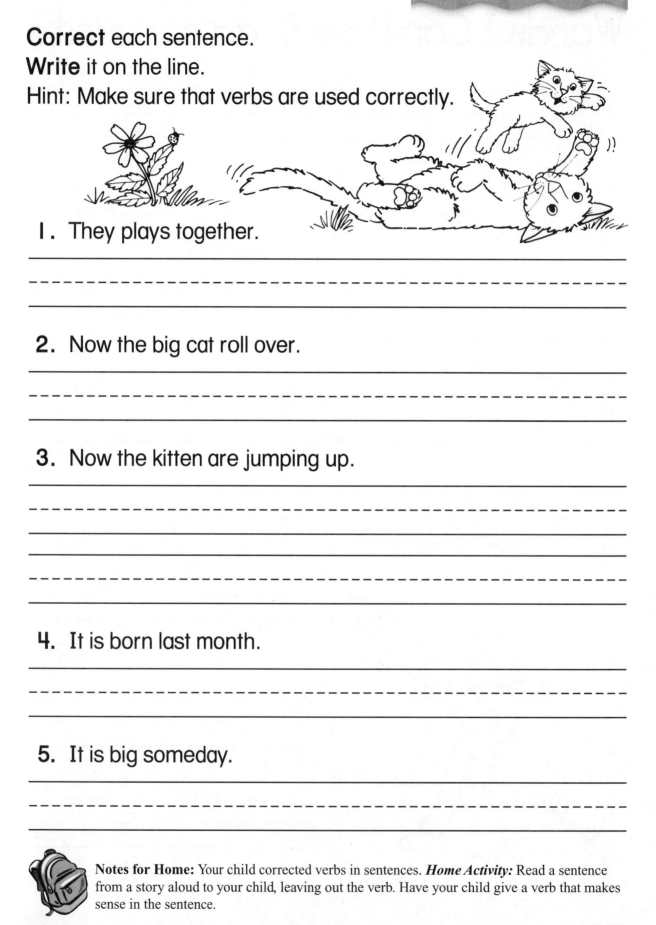

1. They plays together.

_____
- -
_____

2. Now the big cat roll over.

_____
- -
_____

3. Now the kitten are jumping up.

_____
- -
_____
_____
- -
_____

4. It is born last month.

_____
- -
_____

5. It is big someday.

_____
- -
_____

Notes for Home: Your child corrected verbs in sentences. **Home Activity:** Read a sentence from a story aloud to your child, leaving out the verb. Have your child give a verb that makes sense in the sentence.

Name _____

Reading Log

Date	What is the title?	Who is the author?	What did you think of it?

Name _____

Reading Log

Date	What is the title?	Who is the author?	What did you think of it?

Name _____

Reading Log

Date	What is the title?	Who is the author?	What did you think of it?

Name _____

Reading Log

Date	What is the title?	Who is the author?	What did you think of it?